High unemployment among disadvantaged youth is one of the most persistent clouds on the American economic horizon. Thirty-eight percent of all black teenagers of working age are unemployed. In inner-city poverty areas the number has sky-rocketed even higher. Past attempts to assess the causes of youth unemployment in the ghetto have been episodic, frag-mented, and anecdotal. This book syn-thesizes current information on the subject and surveys the literature in three general areas: demography, economics, and anthropology.

As the authors evaluate factors believed to be the root causes of teenage unem-ployment, a harsh, yet increasingly famil-iar, picture emerges. "Perverse population patterns"—white migration out of the cities coupled with an expanding minority population—have created a nonwhite "youth bulge" in metropolitan areas. De-teriorating urban economies are no longer able to adequately support such dispro-portionately large numbers of new work-ers. "Dysfunctional life styles" that pro-vide ghetto youths with the skills to survive on the streets later hinder their chances for employment. In this volume the social and psychological consequences of unem-ployment are discussed in detail, as are the economic structure of the city and ghetto, life styles and career-development patterns among middle-class and ghetto youth, and job-search behavior among teenagers.

POLICY STUDIES IN EMPLOYMENT AND WELFARE NUMBER 33

General Editor: Sar A. Levitan

COMING OF AGE IN THE GHETTO

A Dilemma of Youth Unemployment

A Report to the Ford Foundation

Garth L. Mangum
and Stephen F. Seninger

The Johns Hopkins University Press, Baltimore and London

The Johns Hopkins University Press, Baltimore, Maryland 21218
The Johns Hopkins Press Ltd., London

Library of Congress Catalog Number 78-8422
ISBN 0-8018-2125-8

Library of Congress Cataloging in Publication data will be found on the last printed page of this book.

Contents

Tables

Figures

Acknowledgments

This monograph was prepared under a grant from the Ford Foundation to the Center for Social Policy Studies at the George Washington University.

The authors acknowledge the dedicated efforts of LaVonne Booton and Stephen Mangum in searching through the massive literature, with the aid of Andrea Sigetich. Shirley Frobes, James Logan, and Dayle Nattress also provided invaluable research assistance. A number of government agencies, too numerous to mention, generously provided whatever information and data existed and could be identified.

Coming of Age in the Ghetto

1

Youth in the Ghetto Labor Market

Four out of ten black teenagers who seek jobs cannot find them; the ratio is five out of ten in some central city areas. Only 22 percent of all blacks sixteen to nineteen years of age and 16 percent of those living in the poverty areas of central cities have jobs, compared to 45 percent of the entire U.S. population of that age. More than 60 percent of all unemployed black teenagers reside in the central city, with half of this group concentrated in poverty areas. In 40 percent of all black central city families women are heads of households, a status held by women in only 14 percent of white urban families.

However distressing the statistics, they surprise no one. The recital is familiar. The significant issues are "why" and "what is to be done?" The literature has much less to say on the first than the second of those queries. The absence of job opportunities, the corrosive effects of poverty, the excessive availability of welfare and other income maintenance programs, the lucrativeness of crime, the deterioration of the family, are only some causes offered.

The remedies proposed do not necessarily reflect the assessment of causes. A massive "Marshall Plan" for the cities: public service employment, subsidized private jobs, supported work, better schools, rehabilitation of housing, more mass transit, bigger and better jails—all have been advocated. But no really concerted research effort has sought to isolate the causes of youth unemployment in the ghetto. The literature is episodic, fragmented, and anecdotal.

This study is designed as a takeoff point, not as a report of new research. The relevant literature was examined to synthesize from it all that is currently known about the causes of the alarmingly high unemployment rates of ghetto youth; this included a vast quantity of data series, research reports, and other literature.

The research is summarized in three broad areas that might be characterized as demography, economics, and anthropology. The result is a harsh picture that leaves little doubt that the basic causes are found in perverse population trends, deteriorating local economies, and dysfunctional life styles.

The postwar baby boom, in combination with major population shifts within central cities, has been a major factor underlying the unemployment dilemma for central city and ghetto teenagers. The baby boom led to an increase in the number of teenagers within cities by the early 1960s, which, in a relatively static urban population during that decade, resulted in a compositional shift toward younger age groups. Chapter 2 examines the nature and magnitude of these patterns. A factor is a declining total white population in central cities, despite a teenage component that grew throughout the 1960s and then stabilized, remaining relatively constant between 1970 and 1974.

Central city black populations expanded over the same period and shifted toward the teen and young adult age groups. This growing youth component in the urban black population led to a greater number of black teenagers (on both an absolute and a relative basis) by the early 1970s. Moreover, these large numbers of black teenagers represented an increasing share of the total urban youth population.

The growing role of Hispanic population groups within metropolitan areas is another major characteristic of urban populations. Population growth rates for this group between 1970 and 1974 suggest an increased urban concentration of Hispanics as well as of blacks.

The labor supply consequences of these population shifts have been somewhat predictable. The number of all teenagers as a percentage of the central city labor force has increased, while the total labor force has remained relatively static over recent years. A larger number of teenagers entering the labor force within a relatively stagnant urban economy has been one factor in the alarmingly high unemployment rates for urban youth. The employment-population ratio is an indication of how effectively teenagers have been absorbed into the labor market. More than 44 percent of all teenagers were employed in the nation during 1976, but in the New

York central city area the figure dropped to as low as 22 percent and was only 26 percent in Washington, D.C.

Urban youth unemployment is overwhelmingly a black employment problem. During the second quarter of 1977, more than 60 percent of all unemployed black teenagers were located in central cities, in contrast to 23 percent of all unemployed white teenagers. These urban youth employment problems are especially sobering when compared to the more favorable patterns in the surrounding suburban ring.

The population and labor force patterns are part of a more inclusive problem that has become known as the urban crisis. Chapter 3 briefly reviews some of the literature on this topic and updates urban employment change into the present decade. The central city's relative share of total metropolitan employment has continued to decline, while overall employment change in the central city has been rather low. Employment by industry and occupation has gained in only a small number of categories, and these have not been sectors that typically employ large numbers of teenagers. Low to negative growth in other categories that are heavy employers of youth is another pattern that is identified and related to high central city unemployment rates for teenagers. These city employment patterns contrast sharply with those in the suburban fringe, where employment growth in almost every occupation and industry has been positive.

Other aspects of teenage unemployment in the city and ghetto are discussed in Chapter 3 within the context of literature on the urban labor market, the bulk of which bears only indirectly on city and ghetto youths. Stanley L. Friedlander's work, one of the few in-depth studies of ghetto youth unemployment, develops a segmented labor market approach to the problem.[1] High ghetto youth unemployment is attributed to an unfavorable industrial structure that offers a net advantage to older workers over urban youth. Other factors such as female labor force competition and high inflexible wages accentuate the youth unemployment problem, although they emerge as secondary to the industrial mix-segmented labor market statistics. Friedlander's work, admittedly limited to a small sample of ghetto areas during the 1960s, does not offer a comparative analysis between ghetto, central city, and suburban areas. It does, however, offer some strong clues that are pursued in Chapter 3.

A study by Sar Levitan and Robert Taggart focuses on the job crisis for black youth and identifies both white and nonwhite urban youth as peripheral workers characterized by intermittent or part-time, low-income employment, concentrated in low-status industries and occupations.[2] A "credentials gap" is blamed as one major reason for the continuing disparity between nonwhite and white employment patterns in that the black youth is more likely to be poorly prepared for and ill-adjusted to the world of work. Levitan and Taggart point out that the substantial gains in educational attainment made by black youth have not brought commensurate improvement in their labor market status. The credentials of black youth are not as respected as those of white youth, a labor market prejudice supported in part by qualitative differences in high school education and by racial discrimination.

Other studies of teenage unemployment deal with the kinds of jobs that teenagers attain in their transition from school to work and with the effect of minimum wage laws on teenage unemployment. Chapter 3 concludes with a discussion of possible linkages between teenage labor force status and family income. Some limited evidence is presented, and the feasibility of measuring the teenage component of family income is outlined.

Labor market successes and failures of ghetto youth are more than a narrowly defined economic phenomenon. Anthropology, sociology, and psychology have their contributions to make in helping to understand the causes and consequences of unemployment among central city youth. Life styles, attitudes toward work and the urban environment, role models, family structure and income, crime and punishment all interact in complex and diverse ways and have substantial impact on the labor market experiences and career development of ghetto youth. Chapter 4 examines the literature and identifies what is known about this extremely complex subject.

Chapter 5 summarizes the findings of the study, extracts its policy implications, and finally achieves the real objective of this work: to summarize what appears to be known about the incidences and causes of central city youth unemployment and to specify needed research to fill in the significant gaps in that knowledge. The end product, then, is a research agenda to intensify illumination of one of the most critical areas of U.S. public policy.

2

Central City Population and Labor Force Trends

Problems of teenage unemployment in urban labor markets are an inherent part of the so-called urban crisis that stems from major demographic and socioeconomic shifts within the nation's urban core. These shifts, in combination with the postwar baby boom, have had significant effects on the age and race structure of central city populations. The pattern of population changes in cities, in comparison to suburban areas, has become part of the standard description of the urban crisis. The following discussion briefly reviews this record and updates the most important trends and patterns into the 1970s.

Stagnant population growth in the inner city, with an increase in the minority component, was a salient feature of urban populations during the 1960s. Between 1960 and 1970 the age composition of urban populations shifted toward the sixteen-to-twenty-four-year age group with a slight moderation in this trend during the first half of the 1970s. This youth bulge in the central city has become increasingly dominated by nonwhite teenagers, a pattern that promises to continue on the basis of differential growth rates in the black and white youth populations. The growing minority teenage population in cities has obvious impacts on the supply side of urban labor markets, an effect that is analyzed from the recent data on central city and ghetto youth unemployment and labor force size.

Population Changes and Shifting Racial Composition

The pattern of population growth within central cities and the changing racial composition of that population have been two of the more dramatic factors in the urban crisis. The overall population growth rate within central cities from 1960 to 1969 lagged behind the national rate and was completely overshadowed by population growth in the suburbs. The nation's population increased by 12 percent during that decade, while central city population increased by only 2 percent. Population growth in suburbia dominated the geographic pattern of demographic change with an overall 30 percent growth rate during the 1960s.

The racial composition of these growth rates, by location, followed a general pattern of negative growth for the white and positive growth for the black populations within central cities. As shown in Figure 1, the population growth rate for central city whites was negative in all central cities, declining at a greater rate in the larger cities.

In direct contrast, black population growth rates were extremely high in central cities during the 1960s. Urban growth rates for the black population ranged from 32 percent in all central cities to 41 percent in large central cities over the decade. This extreme racial disparity in central city population growth was partially offset by the suburban pattern, where population growth rates for black and white cohorts were both positive and high with 37 and 29 percent growth rates, respectively.

These geographic patterns of demographic change have continued, with one or two notable differences, into the 1970s. Although the central city population growth for all races showed positive yet modest gains during the 1960s, it was negative for the period between 1970 and 1974 (see Figure 2). Central city population levels decreased by a small negative rate nationwide, while large central cities experienced a negative 4 percent change in population. The white cohort followed the overall rate with a negative growth rate of 5 percent and an even bigger negative rate in large central cities.

An unbalanced pattern of population growth, by race, continued to characterize central cities into the 1970s. The black population within central cities increased at a positive rate of 6 percent, with a somewhat lower but positive rate in big cities. More recent available

Figure 1. Population Change by Area of Residence and Race, 1960–1969

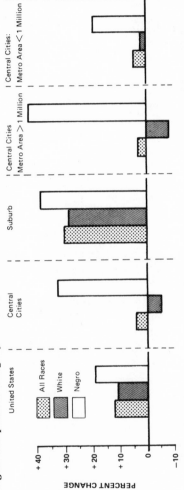

SOURCE: U.S. Bureau of the Census, *Current Population Reports*, Series P-23, No. 33, "Trends in Social and Economic Conditions in Metropolitan and Nonmetropolitan Areas" (Washington, D.C.: U.S. Government Printing Office, 1970).

Figure 2. Population Change by Area of Residence and Race, 1970–1974

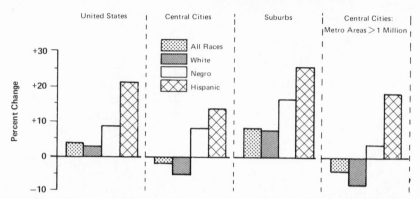

SOURCE: U.S. Bureau of the Census, *Current Population Reports,* Series P-23, No. 55, "Social and Economic Characteristics of Metropolitan and Nonmetropolitan Areas, 1974 and 1970" (Washington, D.C.: U.S. Government Printing Office, 1975).

data on persons of Spanish origin suggest that this ethnic group grew by 14.4 percent in central cities and by 17.5 percent in large central cities. Another significant measure of current and future racial composition of cities is the distribution of population by area of residence and race, as shown in Figure 3.

The American proclivity to reside in metropolitan areas is a well-documented phenomenon. In 1960, 112 million people lived in metropolitan areas, one-third of them in central cities. This residential pattern, however, has displayed striking changes by racial group over the past fifteen years. The nation's white population has become increasingly less centered in the urban core, declining from 30 percent in 1960 to 25 percent by 1974. During that time, the country's black population has displayed a strong predilection for remaining in or migrating to the inner city; 52 percent of blacks lived within central cities in 1960 and 58 percent by 1974.

The Hispanic population has also been heavily concentrated within metropolitan areas, but with a more even distribution between the inner city and the suburban fringe. Approximately half of the 10 million persons of Spanish origin in the nation lived in central cities, while a smaller percentage lived in suburbia during 1974. Because of the relative fewness of their number, however, persons of Spanish origin comprised 7 percent of central city popu-

Figure 3. Population Distribution by Area of Residence and Race: 1960, 1970, 1974

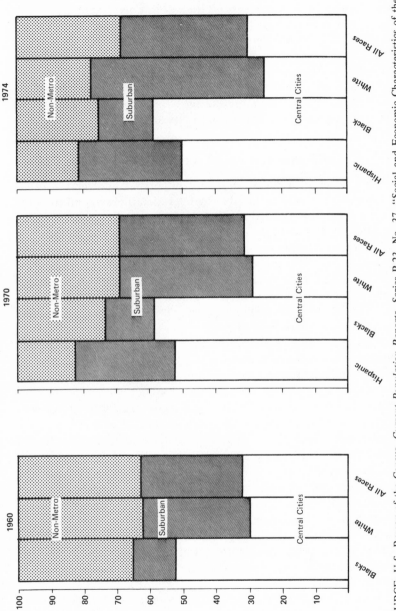

SOURCE: U.S. Bureau of the Census, *Current Population Reports*, Series P-23, No. 37, "Social and Economic Characteristics of the Population in Metropolitan and Nonmetropolitan Areas: 1970 and 1960" (Washington, D.C.: U.S. Government Printing Office, 1971); and *Current Population Reports*, Series P-23, No. 55.

lation in 1970 and 8.6 percent in 1974. This ethnic group was more heavily concentrated in large central cities, where the Hispanic share of total population reached 10.5 percent in 1974. Adding the Spanish population to the black share of 27 percent in 1974 gave big central cities an overall minority population of 37.5 percent. Minorities as a percentage of central city population were above 40 percent during 1970 in Chicago, New York, St. Louis, and Atlanta and exceeded 60 percent in Newark.[1]

Migration Flows and Central City Populations

The increase in the central city minority component between 1960 and 1974 was accentuated by migration flows to and from the urban core. City populations declined by approximately 8.5 million between 1970 and 1974 because of the exodus to the suburbs. An additional 2.9 million inner-city dwellers migrated to nonmetropolitan areas. This gross outflow was partially offset by migration inflows of 3.9 million persons from suburbia, plus an additional 1.6 million persons who moved from nonmetropolitan regions to the central city. Outmigration resulted in a loss of 5.9 million people over the four-year period.

The racial and socioeconomic composition of these migration flows conforms to some commonly accepted stereotypes, although it also offers interesting twists. About 7.7 million white persons left central cities for the suburbs; another 3 million moved to the country between 1970 and 1974. Balanced against this was an inflow of 3.4 million whites from suburbia, along with 1.4 million more from rural areas. Thus the specter of a massive unilateral outflow of white populations from the central city is misleading.

The income levels of families who moved from verus those who moved into central cities do fit the stereotype of deteriorating income levels within central cities. Families living in cities during 1970 had a mean income of $13,349 compared to the $12,864 mean income of those that moved into the cities between 1970 and 1974. At the same time, more affluent families moved out—the mean income for families who moved out of cities between 1970 and 1974 was $14,169.[2]

Blacks have been less erratic then whites in their residential and migratory habits. Although a few more than half a million blacks moved to either suburbia or the country, the majority of the 12 million blacks living in central cities during 1974 were the same as those who had resided there in 1970. Census Bureau estimates suggest that central city blacks are fairly mobile within a given city and that a third of those blacks who moved between 1970 and 1974 still lived in the same central city Standard Metropolitan Statistical Area (SMSA), an intraurban mobility measure that compares to 22 percent for the white population and 25 percent for the total population. The net inflow of blacks to the city was approximately zero between 1970 and 1974, with slightly more than half a million blacks moving into central cities and a corresponding number moving to the suburbs.

These migration flows into and away from central cities are highly aggregated measures that give some clues to nationwide patterns. An equally important mobility factor is the origin of people who live in the central city, particularly those who live in the urban ghetto. Some preliminary estimates of this factor are constructed in Table 1 from 1970 census data for low-income areas in sixty U.S. cities.[3]

Family Status and Sex Composition

Historically, the urban ghetto has been an ethnically rich and racially varied place, a characteristic that seems to hold into the 1970s. A considerable number of ghetto family heads were foreign born, ranging from 18 percent of males to 14 percent of females of all races. This large number was primarily due to the white cohort that had significant concentration of foreign-born family heads. Ghetto blacks are, quite accurately, American Negroes with very small proportions of foreign-born family heads.

A large proportion of black family heads were born outside the urban ghetto, the greater share coming from smaller cities and rural areas. Of the 71 percent of black male family heads not born in the cities surveyed, over half came from medium to small cities, while another third were born in rural areas. They were not recent migrants, however; almost 90 percent of this group had lived in the survey city for five years or more. The rural-urban migration of blacks seems to have stabilized during the 1970s; only a third of the 600,000 black immigrants to central cities between 1970 and 1974 came from nonmetropolitan areas.

White family heads of both sexes had a greater tendency than

Table 1. Residential Mobility of Central City Family Heads in Low-Income Areas, 1970
(in percentages)

	Not born in U.S.	Born in U.S. but not this city	Born in U.S. but not this city — Born in			Lived in this city	
			Lg. city or suburb	Med. and Sm. city, town	Farm and rural	5 years or less	5 years or more
All races							
Male head	18.4	52.4	15.4	54.6	30.0	15.8	84.2
Female head	14.2	53.4	16.1	57.3	26.3	13.8	86.2
Black							
Male head	4.1	71.3	13.9	52.3	33.7	12.4	87.6
Female head	2.7	65.5	15.7	56.8	27.5	11.8	88.2
White							
Male head	28.3	37.0	17.8	58.5	23.4	18.2	81.8
Female head	33.9	30.6	18.9	61.1	20.0	17.0	82.7

SOURCE: Data in U.S. Bureau of the Census, *Employment Profiles.*

blacks to originate in another large city or suburb. The 37 percent of white male family heads not born in the survey city included less than a quarter who had been born in rural areas. In contrast to blacks, these were more recent residents, with 18 percent living in the ghetto city five years or less.

On the whole, this sample suggests considerable stability in terms of urban ghetto residency. A large proportion (85 percent) of family heads of all races, black and white, male and female, had lived in the city five years or more.

The sex composition of total population did not show a strong variation for either race or place of residence in 1970 and 1974. Of the total population of all races, approximately 48 percent of the males lived in the cities and suburbs during those two years, a percentage share that also held for larger central cities and their suburbs. The male percentage of total white, black, and Hispanic populations was also 48 in both city and suburb in 1970 and 1974 for the nation as a whole.

Females as a component of the population emerged most significantly in head-of-household data. Of all central city families, 16 percent were headed by females in 1970, a share that rose to 19 percent in 1974 (see Table 2). Suburbs typically had relatively fewer female-headed families, less than 10 percent of total families. These city-suburb shares are somewhat misleading in view of differing rates of change in families headed by women during the early 1970s. The number of female-headed families increased by 22 percent in central cities between 1970 and 1974, a percentage change that was slightly exceeded by the suburbs, where the change was 26 percent. This difference in growth was even more pro-

Table 2. **Percentage of Families Headed by Women in Cities and Suburbs, by Race, 1974, 1970**
(1970 metropolitan area definition)

| | 1974 | | 1970 | |
	Central city	Suburban area	Central city	Suburban area
All Races	18.9	9.5	15.7	8.4
White	13.8	8.8	12.3	7.9
Black	39.1	25.7	30.5	22.2

SOURCE: U.S. Bureau of the Census, *Current Population Reports.* Series P-23, No. 55.

nounced in big metropolitan areas, where the central city percentage change of 18 was considerably below the suburban rate of 27.

Differences in the sex status of family heads were most significant when families were disaggregated into racial groups. Women headed 12 percent of all central city white families in 1970; the number increased slightly by 1974. Black urban families had a stronger tendency toward female heads, with women heading 30 percent of all black urban families in 1970, a share that rose to 39 percent by 1974. Some of these sex and race characteristics of family heads show up in the poverty data discussed in Chapter 3.

The proportion of both white and black families headed by women was lower in the suburbs. The former had a 9 percent proportion of all families headed by women for the two years, while black female-headed families in the suburbs were approximately one-fourth of all black suburban families in 1974. Thus, the frequently cited trend toward broken families seems to be accurate for the suburbs and even more so for the central city. While no hard figures are available for teenagers and the incidence of separated families, the studies on life styles discussed in Chapter 4 offer some indirect evidence on the family unit and youth behavior patterns.

Demographic Patterns for Urban Teenagers and Young Adults

The postwar baby boom was a second major factor that interacted with the urban crisis to contribute to labor market problems for urban youth throughout the 1960s and 1970s. The annual number of total births increased to a temporary peak (see Figure 4) of 3.8 million in 1947, an upward shift that progressed to a four-year peak between 1958 and 1962 of slightly under 4.5 million births per year. The rapid increase to the peak of 1947 was due to a significant increase in the number of first-born children, while the second peak during the late 1950s and early 1960s was due to second- and third-born children.

A direct consequence of this population boom was an increase in the number of youth entering the labor force by the early 1960s. Significantly larger numbers of teenagers (sixteen years and older) entered the labor force in 1963. The effect of the baby boom was not a one shot phenomenon restricted to 1963; increased entrance

Figure 4. Numbers of Live Births by Birth Order, 1920-1975

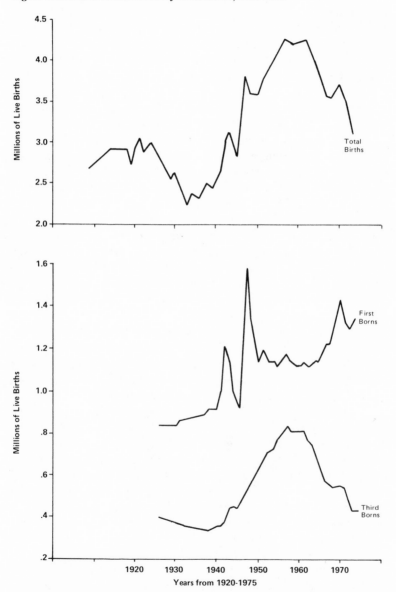

SOURCE: U.S. National Center for Health Statistics, *Vital Statistics of the United States* (Washington, D.C.: U.S. Government Printing Office, 1976).

of teenagers into the labor force continued, essentially unabated, throughout the 1960s and was directly related to the sustained increase in annual total births between 1947 and 1958. Moreover, the four-year peak in total births per annum, which ran from late 1958 to 1962, pushed the boom entry phenomenon into the 1970s and promises to carry into the future for several years.

All of these factors have generated enormous pressures on the supply side of youth labor markets. One manifestation of these pressures is the continued and persistently high unemployment rates for teenagers that have prevailed since the baby boom cohort first struck the labor market in the 1960s. The jobless rate for teenagers increased from a comparatively low 8.2 percent in 1951 to 16 percent in 1974 and climbed to a high of 20 percent in 1975 (aided by the 1974-75 recession). These patterns and trends remained—although in somewhat milder form—for those who became young adults of twenty to twenty-four years of age. While the labor market supply effects were not so severe for the older group, they have figured in the overall pattern of unemployment for the youth component of the 1960s and current labor force. The data in Table 3 suggest a compositional shift toward younger age cohorts in central cities between 1960 and 1970. The teenage share of central city population for all races increased from 5 to 7 percent during the decade, a 40 percent increase in proportion that was matched by the young adult group. Whereas 42 percent of the population was twenty-four years old or younger in 1960, this youth share increased to 45 percent by 1970 in central cities.

The age composition of central city population by race displayed similar yet different patterns over the same period. White and black teenagers as percentages of their respective total populations increased by two points over the decade, a pattern repeated by young adults in both racial groups. On the whole, these relative shifts were greater for black youth (twenty-four years and younger), who went from half to 56 percent of the total black population in 1970. Young whites constituted a relatively constant share of the declining total white population in central cities over the same period.

These same differential patterns were apparent in the median age level by race. Median ages of white central city populations remained fairly constant between 1960 and 1970. Over the same period, median age levels of the black population dropped from

Table 3. Population, Size, and Youth Component for Central Cities and Suburban Areas, 1970 and 1960

Age	All Races		White		Negro	
	1970	1960	1970	1960	1970	1960
Central cities						
Total population (millions)	58.6	57.8	45.1	47.6	12.6	9.5
Percent 16 to 19 years	7	5	7	5	8	6
Percent 20 to 24 years	9	7	9	7	9	7
Median age	30.1	31.3	32.7	32.5	22.5	25.6
Suburban areas						
Total population (millions)	72.9	54.6	68.5	51.8	3.5	2.4
Percent 5 to 15 years	24	23	24	23	28	26
Percent 16 to 19 years	7	5	7	5	8	6
Percent 20 to 24 years	7	5	7	5	7	7
Median age	26.9	28.1	27.3	28.4	23.6	23.1

SOURCE: U.S. Bureau of the Census, *Current Population Reports*, Series P-23, No. 37.

25.6 to 22.5 years. Moreover, this shift toward a younger age structure was for an inner-city population group that grew by three million people over the decade, resulting in a substantially larger black share of the youth population within the nation's central cities.

The suburban pattern of shifts in the age composition by race did not differ significantly from the urban pattern set during the 1960s. However, the absolute number of white youths was a quantum jump above that of black youths. Median age levels, though higher for the whites than blacks, fell for the former and rose for the latter in the suburbs.

The age composition of central cities into the 1970s generally followed the pattern set during the previous decade. Comparisons with the earlier data are complicated by the fact that age breakdowns for 1974 were shifted to fourteen to seventeen and eighteen to twenty-four years of age (see Figure 5). But the youth population of all persons twenty-four years old and younger is still a meaning-

Figure 5. Teenagers and Young Adults as a Percent of Total Population by Residence and Race, 1974

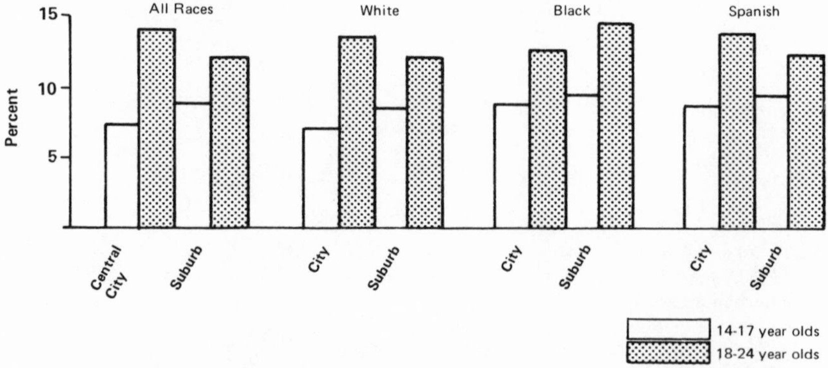

SOURCE: U.S. Bureau of the Census, *Current Population Reports,* Series P-23, No. 55.

ful comparison. That age composition share remained constant for the white central city population. The youth component of the central city black population dropped from 56 percent in 1970 to 53 percent by 1974, although the latter share was for a central city population group that increased by approximately one million persons over this period. The median age of the black population increased moderately from 22.5 years in 1970 to 23.4 in 1974. The Spanish population in 1974 had a youth component of 57 and 58 percent of the population in the cities and the suburbs, respectively, with a median age of 21.3 years.

These changing age compositions for minority population groups, in combination with a declining white central city population, have resulted in greater concentratons of minority youth in the nation's inner cities over the past decade, a pattern that is clearly illustrated for blacks as the nation's largest minority (in Figure 6). Black teenagers, as a percentage of all central city teenagers, increased from 18 percent in 1960 to 24 percent by 1969. This pattern was even more striking in large central cities, where black shares of the teenage population went from 20 to 30 percent over the same period.

The increased concentration of minorities in central cities also held for young adults aged twenty to twenty-four years. Black shares of the total young adult population changed from 16 to 21 percent

Figure 6. Black Teenagers and Young Adults as a Percent of Total Population in Age Category: 1960, 1969, 1974

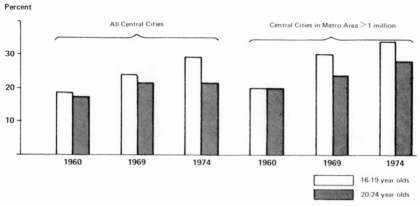

SOURCE: U.S. Bureau of the Census, *Current Population Reports,* Series P-23, Nos. 37 and 55.
NOTE: Age categories are 14–17 and 18–24 for 1974.

for all central cities during the decade of the 1960s. This minority concentration was even greater within big urban cores, where the black share of the total young adult population reached 24 percent in 1969.

This pattern of minority youth concentration on both a relative and an absolute basis continued into the 1970s. By 1974 black youths represented one-half of the central city population within the fourteen-to-twenty-four-year-old age bracket. Moreover, this black share was in a youth population that increased by half a million people in cities during the four-year interval, in contrast to a constant white youth population in the urban core. Black youths were an even larger majority in this same age cohort within big central cities, with a 60.5 percent share in 1974.

An examination of growth rates for these various age cohorts by race suggests a probable continuation of inner-city minority concentration but at a slower pace. The percentage change in black youth age cohorts was positive within central cities between 1970 and 1974, as shown in Figure 7. Black teens, aged fourteen to seventeen, increased at an 11 percent rate over this four-year interval, while the next immediate age group grew by 17 percent. But

Figure 7. Percent Change in Teenage and Young Adult Age Categories by Race and Residence, 1970–1974

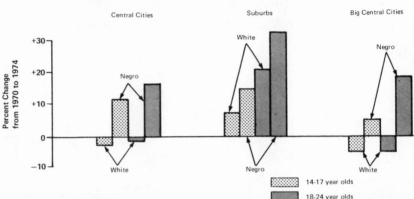

SOURCE: U.S. Bureau of the Census, *Current Population Reports,* Series P-23, Nos. 37 and 55.

in each case and particularly in the big central cities, young adult groups increased more rapidly than did teenagers.

The four-year rate of change for white youths was negative in central cities. The number of white youths aged fourteen to seventeen decreased by 3.5 percent, while the older white cohort declined at a smaller negative rate between 1970 and 1974. These negative growth rates were considerable in the larger central cities, with both rates for the two white youth age cohorts running at approximately 4 percent over the four-year interval.

The suburban growth pattern was more balanced in comparison to that of the inner city. The two youth cohorts increased for both blacks and whites, although faster and in far larger absolute numbers for the latter.

Youth Demographics in Two Urban Ghettos

The lack of mid-decade reference points is a major problem in analyzing inner-city demographic patterns for the 1960s. Extensive and detailed data are available for the end points of 1960 and especially 1970, when a wealth of data was made available (discussed at the end of this chapter). The paucity of mid-decade demographic data is particularly frustrating in view of the timing of the youth growth. It was precisely during the early and mid-1960s that the consequences of this demographic phenomenon began to emerge.

There are, however, some limited data sources that allow the researcher to piece together a rough idea of what happened within central cities during that time. The Census Bureau collected data during 1965 for inner-city areas of South and East Los Angeles and also for a central portion of Cleveland, Ohio. These data, published in 1966, contain comparisons of various social, economic, and demographic factors between 1960 and 1965 for these central city areas. It is possible to extend these comparisons to 1970 for the same two inner-city areas by using the relevant volumes from *Employment Profiles of Selected Low-Income Areas*.[4]

The Cleveland data are the most useful because the 1960–65 inner-city boundaries roughly correspond to the 1970 employment survey area. In that latter survey, twenty additional census tracts were included and combined with the earlier geographic area. Demographic measures for teenagers and young adults in the Cleveland central city over the decade are reconstructed in Figure 8.

The teenage cohort, by sex, consistently coincides with the timing of baby boom impacts, rising to a peak by mid-decade and leveling off in 1970. Male teenagers, as a percentage of the total male population sixteen years and older, increased from 8.4 percent in 1960 to 12.6 percent by mid-decade, thereafter declining to 11 percent in 1970. Female teenagers, as a percentage of the Cleveland inner-

Figure 8. Teenagers and Young Adults as Percents of Male and Female Populations Sixteen Years and Older: Inner City of Cleveland

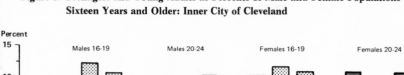

SOURCE: U.S. Bureau of the Census, *Current Population Reports,* Series P-23, No. 19; and *1970 Employment Profiles of Selected Low-Income Areas,* Cleveland, Ohio.

city female population, increased from 9.1 to 11.5 percent and then declined to 10.8 percent for the three years of observations.

These patterns for males and females were matched by those for all teens as a percentage of the population with numbers virtually identical to those of the male teenage cohort. Nonwhite teenagers, by sex, showed the same pattern, although their percentage share of the nonwhite populations in 1965, by sex, were slightly higher in contrast to all teenagers. Nonwhite, male teenagers peaked at 13.6 percent by mid-decade, then dropped to 12.3; nonwhite female teenagers peaked at 12.2 percent in 1965.

The young adult cohort in Cleveland declined and then increased toward the end of the decade. To some extent this was a reflection of greater numbers of teenagers during the early 1960s, who passed into this next age cohort late in that decade. All of this data suggest the presence of a considerable youth component that averaged around one-fifth of the total inner-city population sixteen years and older.

The Los Angeles data show similar patterns over the same period. Youth demographic trends shown in Figure 9 for South Los Angeles center on the predominantly black inner-city area of Watts. The patterns illustrated in this figure seem to be consistent with the Cleveland data and with earlier findings, although a sharper decrease in male and female shares of their respective populations should be interpreted with caution.

The 1970 employment survey area for South Los Angeles differed considerably from the 1960–65 survey area. A rough com-

Figure 9. Teenagers and Young Adults as a Percent of Civilian Population Sixteen Years and Older: Inner City of South Los Angeles

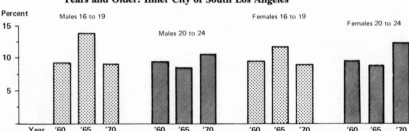

SOURCE: U.S. Bureau of the Census, *Current Population Reports,* Series P-23, No. 18; and *1970 Employment Profiles of Selected Low-Income Areas,* Los Angeles, Area II.

parsion between the two suggests that in 1970 more than seventy-five census tracts were added and some tracts that were covered during 1965 were deleted. Hence the South Los Angeles data are merely suggestive at best, but they illustrate the problem of trying to piece together even the crudest time-series data for central city demographic patterns.

Teenage Unemployment in the City and Ghetto

All of this population growth could lead only to an increased size in the teenage labor force on both an absolute and a relative basis. The number of central city teenagers in the labor force increased by 25 percent between 1970 and 1976, reaching a level of 2.3 million persons (see Table 4). This increase was also reflected on a relative basis, with central city teenagers as a percentage of the urban labor force reaching a high of 8.3 in 1976, up from 5 percent in 1970. Moreover, both these absolute and relative gains by teenagers occurred in a static situation of virtually zero growth in the overall urban work force. This teenage surge on the supply side of urban labor markets was not matched by increased jobs on the demand side. Central city employment opportunities continued to deteriorate into the 1970s, with low and in some cases negative growth rates, as Chapter 3 shows.

This imbalance between supply and demand in urban labor markets has led to the chronically high teenage unemployment rates in the nation's central cities, which is a major focal point for current public policy. Central city teenagers have experienced higher jobless rates than those in the nation, in suburbs, and in nonmetropolitan areas over the past five years. This alarmingly high geographic disparity is even more pronounced in poverty neighborhoods located within metropolitan areas.* Teenage unemployment rates for this geographic breakdown have been 30 percent and higher over the past three years, while the minority teenage unemployment rate in these poverty areas has been running above 40 percent.

Teenage labor force participation and unemployment rates (Table 4) varied for different youth cohorts both within cities and

---

*Poverty areas consist of all census geographic divisions in which 20 percent or more of the residents were poor according to the 1970 census.

between cities and suburbs. Within central cities, white teenagers had significantly higher participation rates and lower unemployment rates than did black youths, a differential that was also true of teenage unemployment rates by sex. White males had a participation rate of 60 percent in cities, approximately 20 percentage points above the rate for black male teenagers. At the same time, the unemployment rate for black male teenagers was double the jobless rate for white urban youths, a black/white ratio that has become endemic in all types of areas and for all age and sex groups during the past fifteen years. White female teenagers also had a participation rate that was double that of black females, and an unemployment rate that was half that of black females.

These persistent differences between white and black teenagers of both sexes might raise the questions whether the central city has such a high unemployment rate because so many black teenagers live there (in 1976 black teenagers represented 19 percent of the urban teenage labor force, in contrast to a 4 percent share in the suburbs, shares that were essentially the same in 1974 and 1975), whether black teenagers experience high unemployment rates because so many of them live in central cities, or whether the overall unemployment rate of which both blacks and teens appear to experience a fairly fixed multiple is the major explanatory variable.

Feldstein[5] analyzed the white teenage unemployment rate in relation to the jobless rate for males twenty-five years and older and identified an initial white teenage rate of 10 percent, which increased proportionately (factor of 1) with the male adult unemployment rate. A similar specification for nonwhite teens generated a much higher initial unemployment rate of 24 percent, which was not statistically related to the adult unemployment rate. He concluded that nonwhite teenagers have high unemployment rates independent of labor market conditions. Gallaway[6] arrived at similar conclusions, with a different model specification. Smith[7] offers more encouraging numbers, although his overall conclusion is not optimistic. He simulates a favorable macroeconomic environment up to 1980 in which an estimated teenage unemployment rate drops to 13 percent, a rate that would still be indicative of a weak teenage labor market, since the youth jobless rate would be triple the adult rate.

The central city, however, clearly has an independent impact. Central city unemployment rates are higher than those in the

24

Table 4. Labor Force Status of Teenagers, by Sex, Race, and Type of Area, 1976
(Numbers in thousands, annual averages)

Area and Employment status	All teenage workers		Males		Females	
	White	Black	White	Black	White	Black
Central Cities						
Civilian noninstitutional population	3,178	1,245	1,567	594	1,611	651
Civilian labor force	1,802	443	948	236	854	207
Participation rate	56.7	35.6	60.5	39.7	53.0	31.8
Employed	1,464	256	756	138	706	118
Unemployed	338	188	191	98	147	89
Unemployment rate	18.8	42.4	20.1	41.5	17.2	43.0
Not in labor force	1,376	802	619	357	758	444
Suburbs						
Civilian noninstitutional population	6,149	402	3,046	190	3,104	213
Civilian labor force	3,631	167	1,903	85	1,728	82
Participation rate	59.1	41.5	62.5	44.7	55.7	38.5
Employed	3,015	103	1,570	50	1,447	52
Unemployed	617	64	334	34	283	30
Unemployment rate	17.0	38.3	17.6	40.0	16.4	36.6
Not in labor force	2,158	236	1,143	106	1,374	130

SOURCE: Diane Westcott, "The Nation's Youth: An Employment Perspective," *Worklife* 2, No. 6 (June 1977): 13-19.

suburbs for all teenage workers, controlled by race and sex (Table 4). White urban male youths have unemployment rates greater than their suburban counterparts, as do black male teenagers, white females, and black females. Moreover, these urban-suburban differences were even more pronounced in 1975, especially for black male teenagers, when the central city unemployment rate of 45 percent was 10 percentage points above the suburban rate for this same sex and race cohort. This consistently higher unemployment rate of 45 percent was 10 percentage points above the suburban rate for this same sex and race cohort. These consistently higher unemployment rates in city over suburb warrant a closer examination, particularly in the context of urban-suburban differentials in overall economic performance during the 1970s as treated in Chapter 3.

Another dimension of urban youth unemployment is the pattern between central cities and the poverty areas within the central city. Teenage unemployment rates have traditionally been higher in central city ghettos than in any other geographic area, a locational disparity that is substantiated by 1970 data (see Table 5). Unemployment rates for male teenagers in the ghetto were double those in the central city, while this city-ghetto disparity was a factor of 3 for female teenagers in the urban ghetto. This pattern holds true for all teenagers—blacks, Hispanics, males, females.

One unusual and, at this point, inexplicable pattern is the higher labor force participation rate for ghetto teenagers over their citywide counterparts. Male and female ghetto teenagers had higher participation rates, according to the census data contained in Table 5. This labor supply pattern for ghetto teenagers is counter to the conventional wisdom that suggests a lowering of youth participation rates from suburban to central city to ghetto areas. An initial approach to analyzing this pattern will have to await the review of the literature on ghetto economies in Chapter 3.

The labor force and school enrollment status of ghetto teenagers is one final characteristic worth noting. The sample of sixty urban ghettos in Table 5 included about a million teenagers. Some of these were either (1) in school and out of the labor force, (2) in both school and the labor force, or (3) out of school and in the labor force. Another portion of the teenage noninstitutional civilian population was not in any one of the above three categories. A little more than a hundred thousand teenagers in this sample were

26

Table 5. Teenage Unemployment and Labor Force Participation Rates, 1970

Sex and age	Central cities				Sixty urban ghettos		
	All races	White	Black	Spanish	All races	Black	Spanish
Male teenagers							
LFPR,* 16–19	45.5	48.3	36.3	43.9	52.2	49.7	52.5
Unemployment rate, 16–19	13.6	11.8	22.4	14.5	28.9	35.1	24.8
Female teenagers							
LFPR, 16–19	36.5	39.3	27.4	30.9	39.2	36.7	33.3
Unemployment rate, 16–19	11.7	9.8	20.4	16.1	29.5	37.9	26.4

SOURCE: U.S. Bureau of the Census, *Current Population Reports*, Series P-23, No. 55; and *1970 Employment Profiles of Selected Low-Income Areas*, United States Summary—Urban Areas.

*Labor force participation rate.

not in school, nor were they in the labor force. Subtracting the 83,000 females from this group (on the possible basis of marital status) leaves a residual of 21,000 males who may very well represent the hard-core ghetto youth discussed in Chapter 4.

School enrollment status raises the broad and complex issue of educational levels of the teenage population in central cities. Educational levels for the total population reveal a city-suburb disparity—68 percent of the suburban population in contrast to 60 percent in the city were high school graduates in 1974. This city-suburb educational difference also held for the white, black, and Hispanic metropolitan populations during that year. And while it is impossible to infer the relative quality of education from such aggregate data, there is some evidence to suggest inadequacies in the quality of public school education.

The credentials gap identified by Levitan and Taggart[8] lends support to this last point by demonstrating that additional years of education have not improved the employment status and earnings of nonwhites as much as they have of whites. Levitan and Taggart argue that most young black males have more education than they need for the jobs they get in view of the fact that the number of nonwhites completing high school has increased at a faster rate than the number working in occupations that normally require a diploma. Bernard Anderson cites recent Philadelphia data that showed that about 40 percent of the high school graduates failed to attain a tenth-grade level of literacy. He suggests a mismatch between inner-city entry-level jobs that require a level of education and skills not available among a large number of inner-city youth. He observes that "as a result of such disparities between the educational preparation of youth, and the hiring standards of employers, large-scale unemployment among inner city youth often exists simultaneously with significant numbers of job vacancies in entry-level white collar jobs in many cities."[9] Moreover, any racial disparity in the relative quality of schooling would prevent occupational upgrading of the urban labor supply. An exhaustive study by Christopher Jencks et al. suggests that education is "the best single predictor of both occupational status and earnings. It predicts occupational status far more accurately than earnings, partly because occupations that require a lot of education acquire status as a result. A year of higher education exerts far more impact on occupational status than a year of elementary or secondary education."[10] This study suggests that the effect of education on economic success is reduced when the observations are controlled for family background and native intelligence as revealed in test scores.

A Final Word

Population measures for central cities come from a variety of data sources, almost all of which are put out by the U.S. Bureau of the Census. The following list is biased toward those items that proved useful in outlining central city population trends during the decade of the 1960s and in updating as currently as possible into the 1970s. Most of these references were used in the previous discussion.

The most useful source for data on the American ghetto was *Employment Profiles.*[11] The data in this report are taken from the 1970 Census of Population and Housing, *Employment Profiles of Selected Low-Income Areas,* United States Summary—Urban Areas. The data are generated from the Census Employment Survey, presenting detailed socioeconomic information on employment-related problems, collected in each of sixty urban areas (data were also collected for seven rural areas, although this was not included in the U.S. summary volume). The urban areas were identified first by reference to 1960 census data and subsequently corroborated by a variety of local sources that were likely to contain relatively high proportions of persons with low incomes. The data consist of demographic characteristics and labor force and employment statistics for each race and Spanish-origin group where the latter comprised more than 5 percent of the area's population, as measured by 1970 Census of Population and Housing.

All of the discussion in this chapter focuses on the pattern of central city population change and the supply side of urban labor markets. We now turn to the demand side of urban economies as revealed by the changing industrial structure of the city and ghetto.

3

The Economic Structure of City and Ghetto

The growing youth population (or potential labor force) in the central city is but one part of the unemployment dilemma facing urban teenagers. The urban labor market, Wilbur R. Thompson suggests, "is the main arena in which urban economic issues must be resolved."[1] Moreover, these urban economic issues should be defined from a broader perspective of overall patterns and trends within the central city economy, a perspective that necessarily entails a brief reconsideration of the urban crisis. This crisis has been characterized by a deteriorating economy of stagnant employment growth, particularly in comparison to the growth of jobs in the suburban ring. The record of urban stagnation has invariably carried over to the demand for labor in general and within key industrial and occupational categories. This latter development has resulted in low to negative growth in employment areas that are heavy employers of teenagers, a labor force group that has been growing in cities during the 1970s.[2] The severity and reversibility of this depressed employment situation and of overall urban decline, viewed with varying degrees of alarm, can be related to a number of different factors.

Industry relocation and the movement of jobs from city to suburb has been a dominant issue in the urban crisis literature. An early and classic documentation of this relocation process was the Hoover-

Vernon study of New York,[3] which identified trends that became a prognostication for other major metropolitan areas. The dispersion of manufacturing employment away from the central core toward the surrounding periphery and outlying suburban areas was the major intrametropolitan shift in New York during the postwar era. Edgar M. Hoover and Raymond Vernon offer a number of motivating factors that contributed to this shift, including rising intracity transportation costs, greater availability of land in suburbia, outward migration of skilled labor, and tax differentials in favor of the metropolitan periphery. Public policy instruments such as the Federal Housing Administration and federal highway programs have complemented these factors of dispersion.

An analysis of industry and employment shifts in other metropolitan areas was carried out by John F. Kain,[4] who examined data for the 1950s and early 1960s. His analysis confirmed that there had been a nationwide shift of jobs and industry from central cities toward the suburban ring. The industry sample included manufacturing, wholesaling, retailing, and service groups (the latter was the only one that showed some employment growth in cities). Some of the conclusions that emerged from this study were representative themes of the urban crisis literature. Kain suggests that most central cities were losing both employment and population to outlying areas, a process that was actually accelerating in a number of cases. Moreover, employment growth rates in excess of population growth in the outlying areas implied a spatial pattern of employment opportunities around the periphery—yet a residual concentration of workers still lived within the urban core—resulting in intrametropolitan movement between home and work.

John R. Meyer[5] examined alternative transportation modes within metropolitan areas and identified an increased dependence on commuting by automobile in and out of central cities that has resulted in the now-familiar peak-hour traffic rush. A more direct implication of this transportation issue has been the accessibility of peripheral jobs to the central city labor force, elevating the problem of movement between home and work to a transportation crisis that has become a standard subcomponent of the urban dilemma. The question of public transit systems emerged from these considerations as an important policy concern that focused on bringing suburbanites into central city jobs and city workers to jobs in the suburbs.

The decentralization of industry and employment has also stimulated research on the qualitative nature of labor force movements into and away from the central city. Lowell E. Gallaway's[6] analysis of 1960–65 data for the South Los Angeles ghetto suggests an exodus of the more economically fortunate from the central city. This argument is consistent with aggregate data discussed by Christopher G. Gellner,[7] who suggests that rapid growth in the suburban labor force has been accompanied by substantial occupational upgrading. A slower occupational upgrading in central cities along with an inmigration of less-skilled workers leads Gellner to the conclusion that, on the whole, more highly skilled workers migrate from city to suburb.

Employment and population movements as components of the urban crisis have led to a commonly accepted stereotype of the residual population in the urban core. These people have been characterized as low-income, unskilled labor, predominantly minority. The latter characteristic seems to hold into the 1970s. Marjorie C. Brazer tested this stereotype for a wide range of socioeconomic characteristics using 1960 census data. The basic issue addressed in her study was whether the "socioeconomic characteristics of central cities and those of the surrounding suburbs are so disparate as to describe two fundamentally distinct population groups."[8] Brazer's results argue against a strong dichotomy of poor cities and rich suburbs. Ratios of suburban to central city proportions were constructed for forty-one characteristics for both the total population and nonwhites. Only three characteristics showed a significant urban-suburban disparity: the percentage (1) of persons who are nonwhite, (2) of broken families with children, and (3) of families containing unrelated individuals. Other characteristics such as housing, education, occupation, and income distribution displayed some variance between city and suburb, but not enough to support the dichotomy thesis. This city-suburb comparison, however, did not disaggregate the city into urban ghettos, a breakdown that might have generated considerably different results.

Although the foregoing issues are not an exhaustive list, they represent some of the major themes of the urban dilemma. A more complete enumeration would include poverty and discrimination;[9] housing and slums;[10] development potential in the urban ghetto;[11]

the issue of black capitalism;[12] and government policy aimed at urban employment problems.[13]

A number of these issues are covered in one form or another by some of the major spokesmen on the urban dilemma. Edward C. Banfield's controversial book[14] suggests three imperatives as necessary prerequisites to an understanding of the urban crisis. The first is demographic—urban population growth can occur either by increased density within the core or by lateral expansion toward the periphery and suburban ring, which seems to be the more usual type of population change. A second, technological imperative conditions the feasibility of transporting people outward toward the suburbs. The third imperative is an unbalanced distribution of wealth and income such that some people can afford new housing in the suburban ring and are able to absorb the costs of commuting to the core in order to work. Together, these three imperatives operate as inexorable forces on the decentralization of population and economic activity from the urban core. This logic of metropolitan growth also generates an inevitable lower class within the urban ghetto, a disquieting conclusion that Banfield[15] continues to maintain in a revised edition of his book.

Bennett Harrison offers a more recent and somewhat less pessimistic view that suggests a normal maturation process for cities caught up in the urban crisis. He interprets the gradual decentralization of urban population and employment as "a normal aspect of mature urban development, rather than a socially pathological phenomenon."[16] Central city economies, in his view, are considerably more viable and have greater prospects than critics of the inner city have assumed.

Anthony Downs[17] accepts the urban crisis as a reality, although he offers a somewhat different perspective: city-suburb disparities in demographic and economic growth are essentially problems of coordinating two different types of growth phenomena. On the one hand, there is a frontier of deterioration in older central cities, characterized by most of the issues and trends discussed earlier. At the same time, there is a frontier of growth on the periphery of built-up portions of metropolitan areas. Any policy approach to the urban crisis must capitalize on the net advantage offered by these two factors.

William C. Baer[18] presents the harshest view of urban demise with a suggestion of terminal illness or death as an inevitable characteristic of parts of the nation's older cities. He attributes urban death to a fairly conventional list of factors that include physical deterioration of the urban capital stock, negative investment via deferred maintenance expenditures by inner-city property owners, and the migration of affluent whites to the suburbs. The efficacy of government programs becomes dubious in this context, since these public-sector actions typically stop short of recognizing urban death as the ultimate terminal point for urban deterioration. From this perspective, selective rehabilitation of urban areas and neighborhoods that are farthest from "death" emerges as a policy strategy.

Central City Economies in the 1970s

The first half of this decade has been characterized by high unemployment in central cities for the total labor force and especially for the teenage labor force. Unemployment rates for the latter have ranged from 19 percent in 1973 to 23 percent during the first quarter of 1977. Moreover, these central city unemployment rates for teenagers have been at least 4 percentage points higher and, at times, 6 points higher than the suburban teenage unemployment rate.

That some aspects of this problem are unique to youth has been effectively argued elsewhere.[19] That some also reflects the plight of central city economies has likewise been documented.[20] The continuation of the urban crisis into the present decade merits more discussion.

Most of the previous literature cited discusses the urban crisis in the context of data from the 1950s and early 1960s. A more recent study by Harrison[21] cites results that extend the economic patterns and trends to the mid- and late 1960s. Those results suggested a slowdown in the rate of urban decline, particularly as measured by central city employment, which seemed to be increasing between 1963 and 1967. Average annual rates of employment growth in thirty SMSAs were negative in the manufacturing and wholesale sectors between 1958 and 1963, but moderately positive (.9 and 1.1 percent, respectively) between 1963 and 1967, years of overall expansion in the national economy.

Over the same two periods, some cities that had experienced

decline began to show economic growth. Of thirty central cities, nineteen experienced manufacturing employment declines between 1958 and 1963; for the 1963–67 interval, nine of the thirty were still experiencing declines. Wholesale employment declined in seventeen cities for the earlier period; this was reduced to ten cities during the 1963–67 interval. A similar pattern held for total employment growth. Fifteen central cities experienced decreases in total employment during the late 1950s and early 1960s, while five of the same thirty were characterized by decreased total employment between 1963 and 1967. [22]

These encouraging patterns for the mid-1960s also show up for specific SMSAs. New York and Philadelphia, for example, had positive employment growth between 1965 and 1967, as did the smaller cities of Denver and St. Louis. The relative disadvantage of the central cities had not ended, however, and suburban areas generally expanded at rates of growth above those of the central cities.

Economic data suggest a continued dominance in both share of and growth in employment by the suburban fringe into the 1970s. Census data[23] for 1974 was used to compute growth rates and employment shares between 1970 and 1974. [24]

Central city shares of metropolitan employment by industry for 1970 and 1974 displayed a continued decline relative to the suburban part of the nation's SMSAs. Total employment shares decreased by 3.5 percentage points during this four-year interval, while employment shares in the construction, transportation-communications, retail trade, and professional service industries all dropped by 4 percentage points or more. Share declines in other industries were a little lower, ranging from 2.9 points in wholesale trade to 3.5 points in the finance, insurance, and real estate sectors. The service sector showed some of the largest declines in employment shares with personal services and entertainment and recreation services experiencing the largest decreases in employment share of all industrial categories.

This relative employment disparity between city and suburb can also be seen in absolute changes by industry between 1970 and 1974. Total employment in all metropolitan areas increased by almost 11 percent over this four-year interval, but it increased at a much lower rate in central cities and remained about constant in large central cities (see Table 6). Suburban areas experienced high

Table 6. Percent Change in Employment, by Select Industry and Type of Residence, 1970–1974

Industry	All Metropolitan Areas			Central cities in Metropolitan areas of 1 million or more
	Total	In central cities	Outside central cities	
Total employment	10.9	2.7	18.1	negative*
Construction	12.8	− 2.0	23.4	− 4.9
Manufacturing	2.9	− 1.0	5.9	− 4.3
Wholesale trade	7.3	− 1.0	13.1	− 1.7
Retail trade	11.9	2.8	19.9	negative*
Finance, insurance, and real estate	20.1	11.8	28.8	3.0
Personal services	− 34.2	− 44.3	− 20.6	− 44.2

SOURCE: U.S. Bureau of the Census, *Current Population Reports.* Series, P-23, No. 55.

*Indicates less than 1 percent

growth rates in employment, with the suburban fringe in large cities (15 percent change) emerging below suburban areas in all metropolitan areas combined.

A breakdown by industry of employment change shows differential growth in favor of the suburbs for virtually every industrial category. The patterns in manufacturing, wholesale-retail trade, and services were particularly important since these three industries represented heavy concentrations of employed central city teenagers (about 78 percent in 1975; see Diane Westcott's article[25] and the discussion in the following section). Manufacturing employment decreased in all central cities, with a rather considerable drop of 4 percent in large central cities. Central city employment in wholesale and retail trade industries increased by modest rates between 1970 and 1974, although these small gains were completely overshadowed by growth rates in the suburbs.

Employment growth in the service sector was a mixed proposition. Personal service employment decreased in all metropolitan areas as well as in the central city and suburbs. The other service categories showed positive gains but, again, there was a considerable disparity between city and suburb. Central city employment in both construction and communication industries decreased, with much more rapid declines in big cities. All of this suggests a continuation rather than a withering away of the urban crisis, at least when measured by employment change.

Another measure of comparative performance is the percentage change in employment by occupation (see Table 7), which seems to conform to an inevitable dominance by suburban areas. The suburbs experienced positive employment growth in every occupational category, with the singular exception of operatives in large metropolitan suburbs. Central cities fared somewhat less well, with negative growth rates in five out of the ten occupational categories, a pattern that was even more accentuated in big cities, where eight categories recorded decreases. The service category (which is more aggregated than the data on employment by industry) had an 8 percent increase, while the manager group went up by 31 percent in big cities. It is likely that part of this latter increase reflects suburban workers who commute to managerial-level jobs in the big cities. Harold F. Goldsmith and Edward G. Stockwell[26] use 1960 census data to stratify cities by occupation-residence patterns. They identify a "Set IV" typology of large SMSAs (greater than 500,000) in which the occupational elite have shifted their residence to the suburban periphery, although they maintain employment in the city.

Table 7. Percent Change in Employment, by Select Occupation and Type of Residence, 1970–1974

	All metropolitan areas			
	Total	In central cities	Outside central cities	Central cities in metropolitan areas of 1 million or more
Managers and administrators, except farm	42.0	30.9	49.1	31.3
Sales	− 2.4	− 9.8	3.9	− 20.4
Clerical	7.7	1.0	14.3	− 3.1
Nontransport operatives	− 3.1	− 7.8	1.1	− 10.7
Transport operatives	4.5	− 4.2	12.6	− 2.4
Nonfarm laborers	18.6	6.2	30.3	− 1.1
Nonhousehold service workers	27.3	15.6	23.0	8.0
Private household service	9.1	− 5.5	33.1	− 14.6

SOURCE: U.S. Bureau of the Census, *Current Population Reports*, Series P-23, No. 55.

A more direct implication for teenage employment problems in central cities is the growth performance of certain key occupational categories. Recent data[27] show significant concentrations of employed teens in sales, clerical jobs, as operatives, nonfarm labor, and in service categories in central cities (see following section). In these categories employment growth was less than encouraging. Employment in sales and as operatives declined between 1970 and 1974, clerical employment increased slightly, and some growth occurred in the remaining two categories. These figures are for all central cities, but they are even more discouraging when computed for large cities. The category of service workers is the only one that showed positive growth; all of the other teen-oriented occupations registered declines in employment.

These different measures of employment change by occupation and industry are for central city portions of SMSAs and do not directly reflect economic patterns and trends in the urban ghetto. Limited inferences can be made from these central city patterns to what is happening in the ghetto, since most ghettos are located within the urban core. But direct empirical measures of economic trends in ghettos are more difficult to obtain and are essentially restricted to decennial census data.

The 1970 census included a number of surveys designed to measure a broad range of socioeconomic characteristics in the American ghetto. One of the most useful surveys for the present discussion was *Employment Profiles of Selected Low-Income Areas*, which was conducted and made available for sixty major metropolitan areas, and included a U.S. summary volume. The following patterns are illustrative of the type of measures that can be constructed on place of residence and industry of employment.[28]

Employed ghetto males, sixteen years and older, were heavily concentrated in durable goods manufacturing, wholesale-retail trade, government, and nondurable manufacturing industries, with somewhat smaller numbers employed in transportation-communication and construction industry groups. A major consideration determining their patterns of employment, raised by the brief survey of the urban crisis literature, is the relation between residence and place of work. The 1970 data suggest that a large proportion of employed males work at jobs outside the ghetto ("low-income area"). More than 60 percent of the employed ghetto males in durable goods manufacturing worked either in the nonghetto part of the city or outside the city limits; 51 percent were employed in nondurable manufacturing. The highest proportions of within-city employment (low-income, plus remainder of city, plus not available) were in the wholesale-retail, finance-insurance, services, and government industry sectors.

High proportions of total employment of ghetto females (sixteen years and older) were in nondurable manufacturing and wholesale-retail industries, a pattern similar to that for employed ghetto males. In contrast, however, females were more dependent on the service industry categories, although they match the male employment patterns with a high share (19 percent) of employment in the government sector. The female labor force in ghettos shows a greater tendency to attain employment within the city. A comparison between males and females shows higher intracity employment for females, with the one exception of personal services.

It is not clear that the ghetto labor force that works outside the city is necessarily earning higher wages. Sheldon Danziger and Michael Weinstein used 1970 census data to test the proposition that "suburban jobs held by urban poverty-area residents are economically superior to the jobs held by those who both live and work in the poverty areas."[29] Using Cleveland, Detroit, and St. Louis for the sample base, they found that during 1970 a higher percentage of blacks than of whites in the three cities combined commuted to the suburbs to work.

Of the black employed laborers, 51 percent worked in the suburbs; of the white employed ghetto labor force, 40 percent worked outside the city. This same differential pattern between black and white workers also held for each of the three cities separately. Moreover, the ghetto workers employed in the suburbs (henceforth referred to as suburban workers) did not uniformly realize higher wages. Danziger and Weinstein estimated imputed wages for surburan workers that adjusted the suburban wage for personal characteristics and the costs of commuting to and from work. Their analysis concluded that only 52.1 percent of the suburban workers were earning higher wages than they could expect to earn in a poverty-area job, which tentatively suggests that many poverty-area residents are forced to commute in response to job availability and thus must absorb the travel costs.

The Danziger-Weinstein study also generated useful data on ghetto area and suburban workers by industry. They estimated mean values for the industrial distribution of ghetto workers who commute versus those who work in the ghettos of Cleveland, Detroit, and St. Louis. An extremely high proportion of suburban workers were commuting to durable manufacturing jobs in 1970. This was in contrast to the industry distribution of employment for poverty-area workers, who were well represented in durable manufacturing, but also were more evenly distributed over other categories.

Another study of the ghetto labor market by Shane Davies and David Huff[30] examined the effect of accessibility of jobs on the distribution of low-skill, inner-city black employment. They utilized 1967–68 data for the Indianapolis SMSA to measure the relationship between male black employment in low-skill manufacturing and miscellaneous jobs and the percentage of low-skill job opportunities in fifty-four ghetto workplaces. A positive relationship was identified between these two factors, while both distance from ghetto to work and public transit time had negative influences on the percentage of employed blacks. Job opportunities, distance to work, and travel time explained slightly less than 50 percent of the variance in the percentage of employed blacks, a result that led Davies and Huff to a qualitative inference that labor market information available to ghetto blacks is probably of a low quality and insufficient quantity. They make the interesting and speculative suggestion that ghetto isolation affects the black worker's ability to receive, organize, and use labor market information; in general, a deficient cognitive structuring of the physical environment carries over to young black workers in the Indianapolis ghetto. This latter inference was made on the basis of their sample age structure, in which 51 percent of the black males were twenty-one years of age or younger.

Youth Unemployment in the Cities and Ghetto

The problem of urban youth unemployment can be related to urban employment growth during the 1970s, a proposition that is pursued later in this discussion. But this labor demand interpretation is only one possible explanation among several that have been advocated as the basis for understanding high teenage unemployment rates in the city.

A number of factors have been investigated and advanced as the cause of high unemployment for central city and ghetto youth. One of the few in-depth studies of this problem is by Friedlander, who analyzed 1966 urban employment survey data for twelve slum areas, using multiple-regression techniques, and identified a number of factors that were related to high unemployment rates for ghetto youth. The ghetto areas surveyed were Harlem, East Harlem, Brooklyn, Philadelphia, St. Louis, San Antonio, Pheonix, New Orleans, San Francisco, Boston, South Chicago, and West Chicago. Industrial structure of the central city was a major factor in Friedlander's findings, although this was interpreted as operating through age segregation in the urban labor markets rather than being a structural characteristic of labor market demand in general. He found that urban industrial structure "measured by the shares of total employment in each of the major industries accounted for more than 75 percent of the variation in unemployment rates for youths aged fourteen to nineteen, sixteen to nineteen, and twenty to twenty-four."[31]

Ghetto youth unemployment rates were higher in urban labor markets dominated by construction and manufacturing in contrast to markets with a large retail sector, although these results were qualified for the different youth age breakdowns. High unemployment rates for workers aged twenty to twenty-four were attributed to manufacturing dominance of the industrial structure, while teenage unemployment rates showed an inverse sensitivity to the relative size of the retail sector. Construction employment shares "had the largest adverse impact on unemployment for the total youth labor force, fourteen to twenty-four years of age," while other sectors such as finance, wholesale trade, services, transportation, and government were not statistically important in explaining youth unemployment rates.

The negative roles of manufacturing and construction industries were interpreted as being caused by entry barriers and institutional factors that created segregated job opportunities that favored adults over youth. Friedlander's argument developed along lines suggested by dual labor market theory,[32] in which organized unions prevent or restrict the entry of young workers into manufacturing and construction industries (the primary sector). Employers find young workers less desirable economically, a prejudice that, in combina-

41

tion with union barriers, is "reinforced by the dominant value system, which places health and education of children above all else, has resulted in a segregated labor market. The degree of segregation varies among urban labor markets. To the extent that segregation is substantial, youth unemployment will be high." Friedlander's results were for a sample of twelve urban ghettos and were not designed to explain differences between ghetto youth versus other central city and suburban youth labor markets.

This unfavorable impact of industrial mix on youth unemployment rates also implied that a general increase in employment in all sectors will not help to reduce unemployment. Friedlander believes that employment growth in the retail trade sector is the most direct way to reduce ghetto youth unemployment, but this sector did not significantly expand in the cities for his data set of the 1960s and showed low to zero central city growth between 1970 and 1974 (Table 6). Overall employment growth differentials in the various urban labor markets did not help to explain variation in ghetto teenager unemployment rates. Friedlander thus concluded that "the growth of employment per se will not reduce unemployment among fourteen to nineteen year olds residing in slum areas; however, it will reduce unemployment of young adult workers (twenty to twenty-four years old) in slums."

Friedlander examined several other factors that might be related to high unemployment rates for ghetto youth. Variations in labor force participation rates of youth and net migration rates into the twelve cities were related to differences among the ghetto areas in youth unemployment rates, although they were not statistically significant factors. Female labor force competition also was not significantly related to higher unemployment rates for ghetto youth aged twenty to twenty-four but did affect teenagers. His findings suggest that higher female participation rates were significantly related to lower unemployment rates among sixteen-to-nineteen-year-olds because young teenagers of both sexes leave the labor force when faced with female competition. But this trend may be counteracted among older youths by the necessity for many of them to support themselves and remain in the labor force. Other factors related to youth unemployment, but found to be statistically insignificant, include the welfare case rate and payment rate in the different cities, health, crime, and geographic immobility.

Friedlander related high and inflexible wages to ghetto youth unemployment, although he did not view minimum wage laws as an important determinant of this inflexibility. Friedlander's argument followed a segmented labor market approach in which high wages prevent youth from competing with adults for available jobs on the basis of wage competition. Minimum wage laws are an alternative cause of wage inflexibility and teenage unemployment, and more recent evidence suggests that this is an important cause of youth joblessness.

James F. Ragan [33] analyzed teenage unemployment data covering the years 1963 to 1972 and concluded that the teenage unemployment rate in the latter year was 3.8 percentage points higher than it would have been in the absence of a minimum wage law. Disaggregation of this national data showed that male youths were affected more strongly than females and sixteen- to seventeen-year-olds slightly more than eighteen- to nineteen-year-olds, while nonwhite teenage males suffered the hardest unemployment effects of minimum wage laws. This relationship between minimum wage and teenage unemployment has also been identified by Alan Fisher, [34] who estimates that a decrease in the minimum wage by 15 to 20 percent might decrease the teenage unemployment rate by something like 2 percentage points. Fisher points out, however, that elimination of the minimum wage would not be sufficient to eliminate the problem of teenage unemployment, especially for nonwhites.

Education was another element in the youth unemployment problem analyzed by Friedlander. [35] Differences in education levels did not show up as an important factor in explaining older youth unemployment rates in slum areas, although they were significant for teenagers. Friedlander constructed an educational gap measure that consisted of the difference between the education demanded of the labor force and the education supplied by the local labor market. The significance of this educational gap on teenage unemployment was interpreted as a displacement effect, where higher-educated, nonwhite workers either found employment in the secondary sector, thereby displacing other nonwhite teens with lower levels of education, or the higher-educated teenagers became discouraged and stopped looking for work but remained in the labor force.

Recent research by Harrison [36] uses the same data base Friedlander did, but with a more rigorous analytical method, to examine education and underemployment in the ghetto. Harrison's results pertain to employed male adult workers and lend support (indirectly) to the displacement proposition. His findings suggest that "existing urban labor markets underutilize ghetto workers and do not permit these individuals to realize their potential productivity."

Another important in-depth study of urban youth labor markets by Paul Osterman[37] used some unique microdata for the Boston and Worcester, Massachusetts, areas. He modeled the supply side of youth labor markets in terms of the transition from school to work on the basis of moratorium, exploration, and settling down phases (discussed in Chapter 4). The demand side of the labor market was specified in terms of predominantly small firms that provide intermediate "bridge jobs" for central city youth. The firms ranged from local automotive shops to neighborhood bakeries and were not the long-term employers of youth. Instead, they performed an allocative function of introducing youth to a given craft or trade that might lead to permanent and higher-paid employment by a larger firm. This study was a unique approach within the limited literature on central youth labor markets, although it required considerable research inputs for the generation of the microdata.

The factors related to ghetto youth unemployment emerge from these various studies as a complex, interrelated set of associations. A somewhat different perspective can be developed, based on more recent data, that suggests some alternative approaches to an analysis of youth employment problems in an urban setting and can be indirectly related to the economic performance of cities during the 1970s.

The distribution of employed teenagers by type of industry and area of residence essentially follows the city-suburb split of the metropolitan teenage population and of the teenage labor force. Central city teenagers comprised 41 percent of the metropolitan teen population and 39 percent of the metropolitan teen labor force in 1975 and 1976. Central city shares of employed teens in almost every industrial category followed this pattern, the only exceptions being finance-insurance and government, which showed slightly heavier employment shares in the city.

The distribution of employed teenagers among industries within cities and suburbs is another important characteristic of youth labor markets. Data for 1976 (see Table 8) show slightly smaller

Table 8. Percentage Distribution of Employed Teenagers, by Industry, Race, and Type of Area, 1976 Annual Averages

Industry	United States	Total		White		Black and other	
		Central cities	Suburbs	Central cities	Suburbs	Central cities	Suburbs
Number employed (in thousands)		1,723	3,074	1,439	2,936	284	138
Total	100.0	100.0	100.0	100.0	100.0	100.0	100.0
Agriculture, forestry, fishery	4.4	1.0	3.4	1.1	3.4	.7	2.9
Mining	.2	.2	—	.2	—	.3	—
Construction	4.1	3.0	3.9	3.1	3.9	2.4	2.2
Manufacturing	12.4	12.1	12.0	12.4	12.0	10.5	10.8
Transportation and public utilities	2.0	1.9	1.8	1.8	1.8	2.1	2.2
Wholesale and retail trade	43.0	45.6	45.8	47.0	46.1	38.5	38.8
Finance, insurance, and real estate	3.4	5.2	3.3	5.8	3.3	2.8	2.2
Services	21.3	22.2	22.8	22.5	22.9	20.3	20.1
Government	9.0	8.8	7.0	6.1	6.4	22.4	20.9

SOURCE: Westcott, "The Nation's Youth," pp. 13–19.
NOTE: Data relate to wage and salary workers only.

percentage shares of employed black teenagers as compared to whites in manufacturing; this differential by race was comparatively greater in wholesale and retail trade. The most significant difference was in the government sector, where black youths found 22 percent of their jobs as against 6 percent of white teenagers. This large difference may reflect the high growth in public service employment during the 1960s in the nation's cities identified by Harrison [38] and the avowed purpose of hiring without regard to race expressed by government agencies at the federal, state, and local levels.

The relationship between concentration in particular industries of employed urban youths and the growth performance of these industries during the 1970s offers a tentative point of departure for further investigation. Almost 80 percent of employed central city teenagers were in the three industrial sectors of manufacturing, wholesale-retail trade, and services, but this share dropped to 68 percent for black teenagers. Table 6 identified these same industries as either slow or negative growth sectors in cities between 1970 and 1974 particularly in contrast to their growth performance in the suburbs, where growth rates were typically positive and high, suggesting a stagnant industry mix of teenage employment within cities. To be sure, this may not be true for all SMSAs; Roger Noll's [39] identification of smaller versus larger SMSA growth patterns in favor of the former for the late 1950s and early 1960s points out the danger of generalizing over the entire sample of cities. Moreover, these teenage employment-industry growth relations are tentative and can be used only as a reference point for further research.

Similar observations can be made on the pattern of employed teens by occupation in city and suburb. The data in Table 9 show that occupational distribution of employed teens by sex, race, and type of areas for 1976 (the distributions for 1975, given by Westcott, [40] were essentially the same). There were some small, but not striking, differences between the total U.S. distribution as compared to the city and suburban distributions. The major differences in teenage employment by occupation showed up in employment by sex and race.

Male teenagers were more heavily concentrated in blue-collar occupations, particularly as nonfarm laborers, while female teenagers were disproportionately represented in clerical and, to a lesser degree, in the sales categories. Both employed male and

Table 9. Percentage Distribution of Employed Teenagers, by Occupation Group, Sex, Race, and Type of Area, 1976 Annual Averages

Occupation	United States	Central cities					Suburbs				
		Total	Males	Females	White	Black and other	Total	Males	Females	White	Black and other
Number employed (in thousands)		1,751	912	838	1,464	287	3,155	1,643	1,514	3,015	141
Total		100	100	100	100	100	100	100	100	100	100
White-collar workers	31.3	38.5	20.7	57.9	39.3	34.8	33.7	17.4	51.1	33.9	28.9
Professional and technical	2.3	2.6	2.2	3.1	2.5	3.5	2.4	2.1	2.7	2.4	3.5
Managers and administrators, except farm	1.1	1.3	1.9	0.7	1.4	0.3	1.3	1.5	0.9	1.3	—
Salesworkers	8.7	10.1	7.4	12.9	10.7	6.6	9.9	7.2	12.9	10.2	4.2
Clerical workers	19.2	24.6	9.2	41.2	24.6	24.4	20.1	6.6	34.6	20.0	21.1
Blue-collar workers	33.1	30.5	49.8	9.4	30.5	30.0	31.6	51.3	10.0	31.6	33.1
Craft and kindred workers	5.7	4.9	8.8	0.7	5.3	3.1	5.5	9.5	1.1	5.6	2.1
Operatives, except transport	11.5	10.2	14.1	5.8	10.0	10.8	10.1	14.0	5.9	10.2	10.6
Transport equipment operatives	2.5	2.4	4.2	.5	2.5	1.4	2.4	4.4	0.4	2.5	2.8
Nonfarm laborers	14.0	13.0	22.8	2.4	12.7	14.6	13.5	23.5	2.6	13.3	17.6
Service workers	29.6	30.5	28.7	32.5	29.6	34.8	31.8	26.5	38.0	31.5	36.6
Farm workers	4.6	0.5	0.8	0.2	0.5	0.3	2.9	4.8	0.9	3.0	1.4

SOURCE: Westcott, "The Nation's Youth," pp. 13–19.

female teenagers in the city were well represented in the service job category.

The other major difference in teenage employment patterns by occupation was between blacks and whites. The latter were disproportionately represented in sales occupations in both city and suburb, in contrast to blacks. This pattern was reversed in the service-worker category, with black teens more heavily concentrated than white teens.

Urban patterns of occupational change between 1970 and 1974 offer a relevant perspective on these occupational patterns. Sales employment declined in central cities (see Table 7) over this period, especially in big cities, where it decreased by 20 percent, while the clerical category showed moderate to negative change. Blue-collar employment declined in large cities, although nonfarm labor increased by 6 percent in all central cities combined. These moderate to negative growth rates in employment by occupation within cities were overshadowed by essentially positive gains in the suburbs for every occupational category. Gelvin Stevenson's study[41] identified a concentration of white youth in occupations and industries with faster than average employment growth; nonwhite youths were concentrated in slow-growth occupations. This information is relevant to the present discussion because of the large minority youth component in central city labor markets, which in turn are characterized by slow-growth employment on both an occupational and an industry basis.

All of these industry and occupational comparisons show surprisingly small differences between city and suburb. They also identify the kinds of fields in which employed teenagers have a tendency to find work. The occupational-industrial tendency can be linked to overall employment changes in city and suburb, although the inference for teenage unemployment is speculative and requires a more rigorous analysis.

Another way to look at urban, particularly ghetto, teenage employment is in terms of its shares of total employment within an occupational category. Male ghetto youths (sixteen to twenty-one years of age) represented 10 percent of all employed males sixteen years and older in 1970, while female teenagers comprised 13.5 percent of all employed females (see Table 10). These same employment measures for males and females by race were about the

Table 10. Ghetto Youth and Teenagers as Percent of Total Employed, 1970

| | Sixty Urban Ghettos* | | | | | | United States + | |
| | Total | | Black | | White | | Total | |
Occupation	Males	Females	Males	Females	Males	Females	Males	Females
Total employment	10.0	13.5	10.0	11.5	10.1	14.5	6.1	8.0
Professional and technical	6.6	7.6	9.5	7.0	5.6	8.8	1.4	1.8
Managerial and administration	4.1	5.4	4.4	5.0	4.2	5.9	.7	1.2
Sales	13.8	19.2	16.7	19.2	11.3	19.1	6.8	13.4
Clerical	14.7	24.2	14.9	23.7	14.6	24.7	8.1	10.2
Craftsmen and foremen	6.3	8.6	6.2	6.2	6.6	10.5	2.8	4.0
Operatives except transport	10.7	7.7	9.8	6.9	11.8	8.4	8.4	4.7
Transport operatives	5.2	±	4.2	±	8.0	±	8.4	4.7
Nonfarm labor	15.1	15.8	13.3	18.2	17.8	25.0	19.0	11.7
Nonhousehold service	11.9	11.2	12.6	9.1	11.6	15.3	14.2	11.4
Private households	±	4.2	±	2.7	±	16.7	12.8	7.3

* Sixteen to twenty-one years of age.

+ Teenagers sixteen to nineteen years of age.

± Less than 1 percent.

SOURCE: U.S. Bureau of the Census, *1970 Census—Characteristics of the Population,* Vol. 1, pt. 1, United States Summary, Section 1 (Washington, D.C.: U.S. Government Printing Office, 1973), and *1970 Employment Profiles of Low-Income Areas,* U.S. Summary for Urban Areas.

same for black and white ghetto teenagers as shares of the total employed black and white labor forces, respectively.

The computation of employed ghetto youth as a percentage of total employed within occupational categories from special 1970 census data shows a pattern that reflects the central city distribution discussed earlier. Both male and female ghetto youths represented large shares of total employed by sex in the sales, clerical, nonfarm labor, service worker, and nontransport operative categories. This data and that from published Bureau of Labor Statistics sources such as *Handbook of Labor Statistics,* for 1975 is for sixteen-to-nineteen-year-olds and suggest that teenagers find jobs in the occupational categories that have the highest unemployment rates. Male teenagers in 1970 experienced their highest unemployment rates in the operative (13 percent), nonfarm labor (12.5 percent), and service worker (12 percent) occupational categories, the same categories in which ghetto youths tend to find jobs. Female teenagers had the highest unemployment rates in the operative (8.6 percent) and nonhousehold service worker (11.8 percent) categories in 1970, job groups that Table 10 showed to have substantial proportions of employed female ghetto youths in 1970. This might be a simple circular relationship; it may also reflect a cyclical instability factor within certain occupational categories.

Another significant feature of this ghetto data is the absence of any strong stratification in occupational patterns of ghetto youth by race. The proportions (across any row in Table 10) are fairly constant, with most of the variation being between males and females. One final point is the ghetto pattern of youth employment, compared to the national pattern. The last two columns in Table 10 measure male and female *teenagers* as a share of total employed by occupation in the nation as a whole. It is somewhat difficult to make direct comparisons between data for ghetto youth aged sixteen to twenty-one and the U.S. data for sixteen-to-nineteen-year-olds, but the latter data do provide a rough benchmark from which some initial comparisons can be made.

Ghetto youth seem to follow the national pattern in terms of the occupations in which they find jobs. Nonfarm labor and service jobs seem to be youth-oriented occupations, as are the sales and clerical occupations, both in the ghetto and in the nation. The latter two occupational groups had a higher number of youths at work in the ghetto, although part of this probably reflects the age disparity between the ghetto and national data.

Family Income and the Inner City

The issue of youth unemployment has thus far focused on the urban labor market and metropolitan industrial structure, along with industrial and occupational patterns of employed city teenagers. Another aspect of urban youth unemployment is its impact on both the individual's income and the total family income. Some limited evidence suggests a connection between teenage labor force status and family income. Eleanor H. Bernert[42] identified a negative but low correlation between teenage labor force participation rates and median family income, using 1950 census data. John Korbel[43] analyzed 1960 census data in terms of youth labor force status and family income, along with such other variables as educational attainment and geographic region. Labor force status (the dependent variable) was defined as: (1) the probability that an individual will be in the labor force in April 1960, given that he or she did not work at any time during 1959, and (2) the probability that an individual will be in the labor force, given that he or she did work at sometime during the census period.

Korbel's data, stratified for the age group of fourteen to twenty-four years, found the labor status of this group to be statistically sensitive to family income. Youth entry and staying probabilities in the labor force were negatively associated with family income; low probabilities were associated with high family income, while the reverse was true of low family income. This finding suggests another perspective on youth employment and labor participation in the central city and urban ghetto. For it is precisely these areas that have been typified as low-income, poverty neighborhoods, a stereotype that seems to be consistent with available data.

The percentage of all persons in the United States below the low-income cutoff ($5,038 in 1974) was 11.6 in 1974; this poverty share dropped to 7 percent in suburban areas and went up to 14 percent inside central cities.[44] Persons in families with male heads represented 6.5 percent of all those below the poverty cutoff in the nation as a whole, an indicator of family poverty that remained about the same inside central cities but dropped to 3.8 percent in the rest of the SMSA during 1974. Persons in female-headed families had a much greater susceptibility to poverty, comprising 37 percent of all those in the category below poverty-level income. This same measure inside central cities was 41.5 percent, but dropped to 28 percent in the suburban rings. If Korbel's results are applied to the family income patterns shown in Table 11, these poverty figures may imply important impacts on youth labor force status in central city and ghetto areas.

Other measures of income and poverty substantiate this dismal picture of central city poverty. Current Population Survey (CPS) data in Table 11 show the income of central city families to be consistently below that of suburban families. Mean earned income for urban families was $10,450; the mean suburban income level was $12,897. A greater dependence on welfare by urban families is reflected by the higher mean values of public assistance, a source that constituted 6 percent of urban family income compared to 1.6 percent for suburban families.

Family income patterns in the ghetto display a strong dependence on earned income, although other sources are important. Census data for 1970 can be used to construct a frequency count of the proportion of total ghetto families who receive income from different sources in sixty urban ghettos.[45] This data shows that a larger proportion of male-headed than of female-headed families received earned income from wages, salaries, and self-employment. Welfare and public assistance was a much more frequent income source for female-headed families; approximately half of all ghetto families with a female head relied on some form of welfare or public assistance (these ghettos, of course, were selected on the basis of a poverty criterion).

The importance of alternative income sources in the ghetto is dramatically shown by a comparison to the nation as a whole. A much smaller proportion of families nationwide used public assistance as an income source in 1969, the period in which national census data were collected. Ghetto families, however, relied on wage and salary income in the same proportion as did families nationwide.

The most direct connection between ghetto family income and youth employment would be youths' earnings as a share of family

Table 11. Estimated Mean Values of Family Income Sources, All U.S. Families, 1972

	Family earnings		Public assistance		Social security		Total family income
	Dollars	Percent of family income	Dollars	Percent of family income	Dollars	Percent of family income	
SMSA, central city	$10,450	76.8	$216	6.0	$522	8.7	$12,064
SMSA, noncentral city	$12,897	83.9	$ 63	1.6	$442	6.9	$14,325

SOURCE: Current Population Survey data tape, unpublished, March 1973 CPS, calendar 1972 data courtesy of Tim Smeeding.

NOTE: Percentages do not total to 100 due to omission of some income sources.

income. One possible source of this measure that merits more investigation is the survey of five thousand American families, a longitudinal study that was initiated by the Office of Economic Opportunity both to complement the Bureau of Census work and to provide a better source of information on the dynamics of family economic status. [46]

The initial sample was composed of two thousand families from the Census Bureau's Survey of Economic Opportunity. The families selected were from those with incomes less than twice the official poverty level of income. An additional three thousand families were taken from the national sampling frame of the Survey Research Center (Institute for Social Research, University of Michigan). Interviews, starting in the spring of 1968, acquired information for 1967. These interviews have been repeated each spring, tracing the individual as well as the family through time. (Although the family was originally the basic unit, it underwent several transformations, often rendering the individual to be the more appropriate unit of analysis.)

Family economic status is measured by the ratio of family money income to a basic needs standard. Family income is the sum of the head of household's labor income, wife's labor income, head and wife's capital income (rent, interest dividends, farm business), head and wife's transfer income, and other taxable income (presumably the labor and capital income of children). The needs standard is obtained by adding to the costs of a minimally adequate diet for the family (estimated and priced by the U.S. Department of Agriculture and essentially dependent upon the size and composition of the family), a figure for nonfood needs that is a multiple of the allotment for food (almost twice), and by subtracting from the cost figure for economics of scale in housing and in other consumption needs of large families. The needs standard, computed from a low-cost food plan, is 25 percent higher than the official federal poverty standard computed from an economy food plan. This standard is then the dependent variable of the analysis, an income-needs ratio.

Economic status is viewed endogenously as a function of family size and composition, earnings and labor force participation, transfer income, income stability, and education attainment. Other exogenous variables can be classified as demographic or environmental. The basic model is

$$\text{economic status defined as } \frac{\text{total family income}}{\text{basic needs}} = \text{function of family size}$$

and compositions, wages received, hours worked, transfer income, income stability, educational attainment, demographic information, and environmental characteristics.

This model is manipulated and often decomposed to form the core of the several studies appearing in Volumes 1 through 5 of the survey, representing the years from 1968 to 1974. While these variables contribute to an explanation of the level of economic status, the size and composition of the family principally affects the trend in economic status. Volume 5 covers 1968-74 and, in addition to the sample of the original households, classifies individuals according to their relationship to the household head in 1968.

The problem with these studies is that any measure of teenage contribution to family earnings is buried and embedded in the dependent variable; that is, in one component of the measure of family income. It appears that no specific work has been done on the contribution of young people in the family to total family income. The basic model, however, can be applied to those who were children in 1968 and have subsequently left the family. Daniel Hill and Martha Hill[47] look at changes in economic status of children in 1968 as a function of changes in family size and composition from 1968 to 1974 and develop a model of children's decisions to leave the family, a decision far broader in scope than a labor market decision. Though potentially available data have not yet been put to use.

Unemployment of central city and ghetto youth is a function of many factors ranging from the effects of minimum wage laws to racial discrimination to an unfavorable industry mix that relegates teenagers to low-wage, unstable jobs in the secondary sector. A dominant factor has been the continued urban stagnation in employment growth during the first half of the 1970s. Urban teenagers find employment in the same kinds of occupations and industries as their suburban counterpart, but they are at a net disadvantage since such jobs have been expanding at a much slower rate in central cities. Chronically high teenage unemployment rates, particularly for nonwhites, have been an inevitable characteristic of urban development patterns.

4

Ghetto Life Styles and Youth Employment

Every other organism but humankind seems to work enough to survive but no more. Only the genus *Homo sapiens*, and very few of them, appears to make work a central focus of life. Therefore, it would seem more reasonable to attribute the commitment to work to cultural factors rather than to some urge innate in the human race. If employment appears to play a somewhat lesser role in the lives of central city youths than in the broader population of the same age, it might be useful to attempt to determine cultural as well as economic reasons to explain that difference. To do so, it is useful first to describe the general cultural patterns from which values and attitudes toward work seem to develop for the majority and then to compare those to patterns evident in the lives of central city youth.

The processes and patterns by which youth develop a commitment to work, decide on what they want to do with their lives, then prepare for those roles and undertake them have been the subject of considerable research and a massive amount of literature over the past quarter-century. More recently, similar intellectual investment is being directed to the lifetime career patterns of adults. Since this literature emerges from research projects, the subjects of which were primarily white and middle class, a synthesis of it supplies a useful norm against which to compare what little is known about the patterns experienced by those who grew up in a central city.

Career Development among the Middle Class

Most of the major theorists in the field of vocational psychology view career development as a lifelong process that can be understood as a sequence of stages consisting of vocational development tasks.[1] The career development process interacts with biological and psychological growth and development and comprises part of the broader growth and maturation process of each individual. Career development deals with the self-concept, the formulation and implementation of values, personality, physical strength, and muscular coordination. At the center of the idea of career development is the fact that, for many, work is a means of self-expression.

Most of the research done on the career development process has been conducted with students of a variety of ages, but from an above-average socioeconomic stratum.[2] Because most of the researchers were college professors, they have taken the subjects nearest at hand. But for our purpose, that limitation has its advantages. It allows us to trace what is known about the career development process experienced by those most likely to meet with success in the labor market. Then the life experiences of ghetto youth can be compared for at least a partial explanation of the marked differences in subsequent career experience.

Infancy and Early Childhood

Specialists in early childhood education have concluded that most of the average child's intellectual development is predetermined before he or she enters school, by the nature and extent of the stimulation provided in the home.[3] Students of career development conclude that most of the work values and attitudes toward work that will characterize each individual's working career are also determined early in the home and family environment.[4]

Infants' and young children's first teachers are parents and siblings. While learning all of the basics of eating, walking, speaking, toilet training, and so forth, children are also absorbing the values of those who guide and thus influence them.

The initial tasks of childhood are to survive and to get food, shelter, comfort, and protection. Experience of self and environment is in terms of pleasure and pain.[5] A child develops an orientation toward the environment in terms of the degree to which it meets or fails to meet her or his basic needs. Genetic inheritance also plays a part in how the child experiences self and environment. If a child is born with a physical impairment, such as poor eyesight or a hearing disability that is not detected until the child is older, the degree to which others can create a positive or negative environment is limited. This discussion focuses on environmental forces that can be controlled.

Assuming that the child's needs are met, each experiences herself or himself as successful and the environment as nonthreatening. An early awareness of self and environment as positive and pleasurable is formed. At this stage, some of the groundwork for later development and formulation of personality and self-concept is accomplished. It is too early to experience an awareness of self-expression through work, but some of the antecedents of one's orientation toward work are formed.

In the interval between this early stage and the time school starts, the child becomes more actively involved with the environment. Many physiological changes have occurred that enable the child to walk, hold objects, communicate verbally, tie shoes, button clothing, and throw a ball. Changes in self-concept and personality are reflected in play activities. By observing children at play, imitating their elders, we witness an emerging awareness of the adult world.[6] An awareness of the adult occupational world also becomes evident. The interminable question—What do you want to be when you grow up?—begins to have some meaning to a child.

At this point, the child's understanding is at the fantasy level.[7] Choice in the sense of conscious recognition and evaluation of alternatives derived from assessment of one's experiences, interest, and abilities has not occurred. We can infer that some positive and/or negative value has been attributed to certain adult roles and that the child's fantasy has evolved as a consequence of the things he or she is exposed to at home and on TV. If parents react positively to the prospect of going to work each day and if going to work occupies a major place in the morning's activities, the child recognizes this and is likely to see work as having meaning and significance in life.

The average middle-class child has two parents to whom work

is important and often challenging. They are engaged in professional, technical, managerial, skilled, or higher-level clerical, sales, and service jobs. There is an employed father, who is reasonably successful at his work, invests a certain amount of time and energy in it, and probably enjoys it. The mother may also be employed; if so, it may be as much for the challenge as for economic necessity. Whether or not she is employed, cleanliness and orderliness is important to her, and she probably works hard at keeping her home clean and orderly.

A sense of security and self-worth is vital to the child's development. Children are likely to be expected to put away toys and at an early age are often exposed to the discipline of piano lessons, dancing lessons, and so forth; later they are expected to do homework and get good grades. Without formal instruction, the child absorbs the idea that work is necessary, important, and usually rewarding. Generally positive work values and attitudes toward work are developing.

Later Childhood

At the age of four or five, the child is ready to start school. The impact of the education process on career development becomes important and remains so for the rest of one's working and nonworking life. In the three or four years remaining of childhood and through preadolescence, the child discovers that he or she does some things better than others; that some activities more than others are rewarded by peers, adults, and society in general; and that certain kinds of activities are personally rewarding.

As the child develops the basic life skills, he or she is able to look outward and begins to become aware of a larger world—first parents, then siblings, then other relatives, neighbors, the school, and the community at large. It is a time of awakening awareness of external influences, for all about the child are people working, to whom work appears to be important. In addition, the child gradually becomes aware that their work is important to others because, through work, we serve each other and create a viable society. Employment, including self-employment, is the only apparent source of income. Everyone works or shares the income of someone who does. No other means of subsistence is apparent. The child becomes aware of employment as an eventual personal destiny and begins to fantasize in more specific occupational terms: What am I going to be when I grow up?

The stimuli from the new school environment demand new behaviors, change, and adjustment. The child learns to modify certain behaviors, to delay gratification of needs, and to accommodate the needs of peers and still satisfy the need for self-expression. The self-concept changes and grows. Self becomes more distinguished from other, and fantasy life becomes distinguished from reality.[8] Play takes on a purposeful dimension. Play for play's sake disappears. It is now a means of achieving, of forming relationships, of testing abilities. The new environment presents new role models: the teacher, the policeman who helps the children across the street every day, the fireman who talks to the class about safety, the school janitor, the counselor, the nurse. The world of occupations takes on new dimensions. Occupational preferences usually change many times as the child discovers new likes and dislikes. Career development theorists speak of this as the stage of career awareness.[9]

Preadolescence

At about eight to twelve years of age, the child turns inward again for self-examination in relation to the broadening perceived world: Who am I? What am I like? What can I become? What would I like to be like? Because the child is no longer secure in the loving cocoon of the home and family, a feeling of self-worth, of respect from peers, teachers, and others becomes vital to self-respect, security, and normal development. Success in studies and in social contacts offers evidence of self-worth. The extent and nature of growth is in large part a function of the environment insofar as it provides opportunities for guided exploration and experimentation. This was also the case in the early childhood years, but as each child matures it becomes a more persuasive force in forming future life styles and vocational patterns, because environmental forces can be motivators or deterrents to achievement of occupational goals.

Nearly everyone whom the middle-class adolescent knows in the adult world bases a sense of self-worth on his or her work role, whether in employment, in homemaking, or in an avocational accomplishment. Work is perceived as a source of self-respect.

Along with exploration of self, the adolescent tentatively explores alternative life styles in search of the one that seems to promise the greatest satisfaction. He or she tends to perceive that some occupations are compatible with any particular life style and some are not. Career exploration begins, but it is more in the negative sense of rejecting occupations not consistent with the life style vision. The individual is more likely to decide what not to be than what to be at this point. Whatever the goal, for the middle-class pre-adolescent work usually appears to be an important means to the goal. And within the scope of the occupations of parents, relatives, and neighbors, most of the challenging and remunerative alternatives of the career world emerge. The occupational horizons of our average middle-class child are fairly broad, though still limited to the scope of the family, school, and social environment.

The distinction between reality and fantasy is developed enough that some compromise has been made between what the child wants and what she or he can reasonably attain. As recognition of the approaching biological, physiological, and emotional changes associated with adolescence grow, the time dimension becomes a consideration, although its impact is more strongly felt in the adolescent years. By the time the child is twelve years old, some experience in the work world has usually been acquired by helping out at home, by involvement in a church, school, or community project, by spending time at summer camp, or by shoveling the neighbor's walks in the winter for extra spending money. These experiences provide the young person with exposure to such work-oriented values as work as a way of performing a service for others, of contributing to the well-being of a group, of meeting the expectations of a boss, of being subject to another's approval, and as a task one is responsible for starting and completing within a certain period of time.

Adolescence

Adolescence is a period of extremes, intense emotional highs and lows, and inordinate physical changes. It is now time for children to test the values of parents and society that until now have been accepted and finally to adopt as their own the set of values that have been largely preformed or to reject them for those adopted from external forces. From the instability and turmoil, a stable self-concept emerges for most people. In the process of reconciling opposing values, the adolescent finds an emerging self with a set of values she or he owns that guide present and future choices, including occupational choices, and that determine the ease or rigidity with which future changes in work life are accepted or adjusted to. [10] The implementation of general values and work values is essential to the successful resolution of the developmental tasks of this period.

Adolescence is also a period of testing perceptions of realities, personal and societal values and norms, and occupational preferences in the work world.

Now decisions begin to emerge for the average middle-class child. Again, these decisions are more likely to be negative in their context and consequence. They close doors without the child's having made deliberate decisions. A math class not taken closes a door to later access to engineering or a biology class to a career in the natural sciences. Later, a decision to complete or not to complete high school or to go on to college closes or opens other doors. But decisions made develop decision-making skills.

Because the perceived society measures adulthood in large part by ability to earn a living, one of the developmental tasks of adolescence is choosing an occupation. [11] Some vocational exploration and experimentation has been accomplished. Knowledge about conditions of work, the requirements for training and entry into certain jobs, and the kinds of external, financial, and social rewards associated with different occupations is beginning to be of interest. Evaluating alternatives is now necessary to narrow the range of possibilities. For those who do not go on to college, occupational choice is imminent. College allows for two to four more years before a commitment is demanded. Occupational choice begins to be a conscious problem-solving activity, a weighing of alternatives, a prioritizing of general and work values, an assessment of abilities and interests and environmental realities, and a means for self-expression. The adequacy of the choice is a function of how successfully the general and occupational developmental tasks of the earlier stages have been handled. The concept of vocational maturity is relevant to the adequacy of occupational choice. The extent of agreement between occupational preferences and personal characteristics and the consistency of the preference pattern are measures of vocational and general maturity. The extent of agreement often reflects the degree of occupational commitment and is related to the likelihood of accomplishing the occupational goal.

It is also a time for work experience. Few middle-class children finish school without some part-time or summer employment experience. They have access through family and family friends to a major share of the occupational world. They take jobs that, as permanent employment, would be dead ends, but they never perceive themselves as remaining in those jobs beyond the current financial need or period of interest. They have full confidence that better things are ahead and find no shame in a rudimentary but temporary and convenient job.

The majority assume that they will go to college. There are no financial obstacles to their doing so. Most of the jobs held by their role models presume that satisfying rewards come from submitting to the discipline of the classroom, from good grades, from verbal abilities, from diligent practice at music, drama, or athletics. Peers, parents, and teachers all tend to honor them for those same achievements. Decision-making and preparation are under way.

Young Adults

The stage including ages eighteen to twenty-five is commonly referred to as young adulthood, although as is true of other stages, the preceding stage overlaps with its successor. In young adulthood, occupational choice is stabilized and occupational commitment is strengthened. The occupational self-concept is defined and is being expressed.[12] To the extent that the choice has been adequate, the individual is experiencing some satisfaction and reward.

By age eighteen most young people have worked for pay. In doing so they have taken a closer look at the labor market, are more knowledgeable about how it works, about how it is related to general economic realities of supply and demand, about the value attached to kinds and levels of occupations in terms of responsibility, financial rewards, and service to others, and about the kinds of personalities suited to various occupations. They have some knowledge about what is expected of them as employees and as a fellow worker. If the individual has worked on an assembly line, he or she may have learned that fellow-workers respond negatively to efforts at increasing the piece rate, even though the foreman and the company management may be pleased. If the job was waiting on tables, extra effort could be rewarded without infringing on the work habits of coworkers. As a result of experience, of testing one's fantasy of work in the real world, a stronger commitment to some values is formed and a prior preference may be strengthened or discarded.

Those who attend and perhaps graduate from college, extend the time of actual occupational decision-making to the age of twenty-two or twenty-five. Career choices are generally made on the basis of choosing among academic subjects. Each academic discipline is a passport to a wide variety of occupations.

Beyond choosing an occupation, employers must be chosen. Unemployment is frequent in the recurring movement between school and work and among various jobs, but it is rarely perceived as debilitating. The informal access routes through family and friends assure that another job is always just around the corner. Confidence of career success is strong. A specific occupation may not be chosen before age twenty-four; settlement firmly with a particular employer may not occur before age thirty. Somehwere in this age range a spouse is selected and a home established. But the confidence of success in all of these endeavors is high.

These are the stages of career development, the influences that impinge on that development, and the responses thereto. At best, a trial and error exposure under favorable conditions leads to success without fear. But this is the pattern for the most favored. What about those at the opposite end of the socioeconomic spectrum?

Career Development in the Ghetto

As has been noted, the crucial stages in development and perceptual formation occur very early in a child's life; therefore, the early existence of the ghetto child must be explored in attempting to assess how values and attitudes toward work are formed in that environment. As in the case of the middle-class family, what will emerge is a caricature. Every person, every family, every neighborhood differs. Some families manage to maintain all of the standard values of the broader society, despite their circumstances. Social scientists prefer to study the pathologies, not the norms. A review of the literature is likely to paint a darker picture than the average. But, then, this study seeks explanations of pathologies. It should be possible to generalize the environment and its impact; and those who have contributed to the literature concerning the environment of the central city poor have described a career development process, whether or not that was their intent.

The Ghetto Family

Although not written from a career development perspective, the available literature gives ample insights into the deficiency of the home environment in the development of work values and positive career attitudes and expectations. The complexities are intricate—the composite of the ghetto family may be somewhat unstructured and lacking in definite boundaries. From a child's perspective, the parental role may not be biologically defined but, rather, be the result of availability, convenience, or ability. Several different people may function (some temporarily) in the parental role. It is within this loosely formed household that the child forms his or her self-identity—the answers to who each one is and what each is to become are initiated vis-a-vis the other members of the immediate environment. The beginnings of a support system are formed. The ghetto family demonstrates a remarkable ability to adapt and survive in its environment of poverty, but the values it purveys are not necessarily those that make for later career success. [13]

Lee Rainwater believes that this cruical early interaction period may be detrimental and actually hinder the child's mental development and self-confidence: "But in Negro slum culture growing up involves an ever-increasing appreciation of one's shortcomings, of the impossibility of finding a self-sufficient and gratifying way of living. It is in the family first and most devastatingly that one learns these lessons." [14]

A negative labeling process and identification as a "bad child" are stigmatisms that develop early in the ghetto. Overburdened, fearful parents and those seeking escape in drugs and alcohol are not prepared to assist their children to develop a positive self-image.

The culture and environment also burden the child with a handicap that is more visible and that is clearly threatening in a physical sense. The shabby outward appearance of garbage in the streets, windowless gaps, and condemned buildings do not exaggerate the internal setting. Young children are exposed to rats, cockroaches, broken glass, nonfunctioning or nonexistent bathrooms, over-crowded conditions, as well as deficient food and medical care. Even early play mirrors the undesirable surroundings—it is more aggressive, more violent, more defensive than is the play of his or her middle-class counterpart. [15] Young ghetto children are forming self-concepts while their endangered bodies learn to fend off the numerous daily threats of their surroundings. [16]

While exterior conditions are appalling throughout, varying degrees of order and cleanliness exist within households. Since interior neatness is an extension of outside conditions, there is limited incentive for homemakers; in addition, cleanliness is partly a function of how many cleaning supplies and labor-saving devices a strained budget can allow. One intensive observer suggests that the degree of order and cleanliness is related to the extent the female head feels pressed by interpersonal tension and psychic conflicts, which means that periods of disorganization may alternate with periods of order. [17]

Conclusions concerning the ghetto family are controversial. Daniel Moynihan's report held the weakness of the family structure to be the central social problem afflicting blacks. [18] This position is challenged by many authors, including Laura Carper, who both points out some deficiencies in his statistical analysis and argues that it is not the black family per se that is the problem, but the "pathological relationship between white social institutions and the Negro community which has bred the statistics the report cites—from low scholastic averages to drug addiction to arrest records to ille-gitimacy to unemployment rates." [19] She goes on to say that it is not the matriarchal family (which is a cultural formation common to oppressed people—Jewish poor, Irish poor) that is the social problem, but rather a question of politics. Can there be room for the poor to acquire social and economic power? Whatever the relative strengths of the family itself, the consensus is strong that the child is not likely to be provided with a strong self-image or positive work values. Within this family setting, the key influence for these, as for all other children, is generally the relationship with the parents.

The Ghetto Mother

Because the matriarchal role of the black woman has been given much attention, it is important to determine how this role affects her child. Results of research indicate that for the lower-class black woman, the parental role is highly significant.[20] This is true, even though marriage is often viewed not only as negative,[21] but as a potential threat to the parental role. This positive attitude toward the maternal role is interesting, given the fact that lower-class black women experience early and numerous pregnancies (often without benefit of a husband), which contribute to perpetuating the cycle that prevents them from escaping the ghetto.[22] Little difference was found between middle-class and lower-class black women with respect to the value associated with being a mother and the positive aspects of this role. Further explorations of child-rearing practices according to socioeconomic class have indicated that there are similarities in basic values regarding child rearing.[23] Middle-class mothers expect obedience and consideration from their children, whereas disadvantaged mothers expect complete obedience to authority. This method of attempting to control children by appealing to status and authority may be indicative in the child's reactions.

One common technique of control used by lower-class parents (as well as peers) is that of shaming, resulting in development of a stubborn, self-assertive, defensive position in the child.[24] The mother's initial feelings of warmth and desire toward the child tend to undergo a metamorphosis by the time the child reaches the age of four or five; lower-class mothers do not have a deep psychological involvement with their children. This may be caused in part to their inability to protect the child from the harsh realities of ghetto existence. Not only do they fail to provide adequate shelter and support, but they are often forced to depend on the children for help. In cases where the family has recently immigrated from a rural southern setting (and parents lack formal education), a dependency develops as parents become increasingly reliant on their children's relatively higher degree of knowledge and sophistication in dealing with printed material, city people, and decision making.[25] This role reversal strains the relationship; it makes parents feel uncomfortable in their vulnerable position and promotes disrespect and distrust in the children as parents lose esteem in their eyes.

Mothers display different behaviors toward, and have different expectations for, daughters and sons. In general, the daughter assumes a more favored position in the eyes of her mother—the daughter is allowed to assume a more meaningful and responsible role within the household.[26] There are usually numerous siblings to care for, as well as normal household chores for which girls are given responsibility. In this respect, young ghetto girls gain an early advantage in developing self-confidence and a sense of worth. This favoritism continues in the sense that girls receive more encouragement from others to pursue education and job skills. Very often, when the ghetto teenager has a baby, her mother assumes responsibility for the child so that the daughter can resume her education.

In contrast, the mother's attitude toward her son is more negative and definitely less inspirational. The black male is not given household responsibilities in his early life; therefore he lacks an opportunity to develop self-worth and self-discipline. Perhaps more significant is the mother's inability to treat him in isolation; instead, her treatment is a manifestation of the attitude she has developed toward men. She sees in her son the father who did not provide physical and mental support; the lover(s) and husband(s) who took strength and resources from her, then left her for another relationship. This verbal account from a ghetto mother is revealing: "Lilly also sees in Jerry his father's evils. At the age of nine he is, in his mother's eyes, already a little man who must be prevented from stepping into his father's shoes."[27]

This attitude inhibits growth and forces the boy into undesirable behavior—he turns to his peers and the street, where he gains acceptance and learns that deviant behavior is a means of achieving a positive labeling. The verbal game, "Playing the Dozens," which consists of a continual diatribe of degradation and abuse toward mothers,[28] is one mechanism of release used by ghetto boys. David Schulz sees the boy as having no alternative in his struggle to become a man.[29] In order to achieve his identity, he turns away from a rejecting mother, earns a reputation in the street, and develops the identity he was unable to achieve as a respected member of a household.

This is the view most prevalent in the literature. In one opinion directly in conflict, Robert Staples, in "The Myth of the Black Matriarchy," says that "if a preference is shown for any sex-role in the black family, it would more likely be expressed in favor of the male child. The problems of raising a black male child in a racist society have been great. Many black mothers out of fear—real or fancied—repressed the aggressive tendencies of their sons in order to save them from the white man's chopping block."[30] He views the research that concludes female favoritism by mothers as part of the process of white social science attempting to dichotomize the relationships of blacks. Nevertheless, the overwhelming tenor of the research appears to support as a conclusion the degradation of the male role.

The Ghetto Father

The ghetto father is pictured in the research literature as a nebulous creature.[31] It is known that divorce rates and father absenteeism are high among ghetto males; it is also documented that the lack of presence of a father figure is a significant factor in a boy's behavior in areas of school attendance, attitude, and achievement, self-respect, work attitudes, and crime.[32] The pattern is circular. The male-dominance role is suppressed; he is not a viable, consistent wage earner; he cannot present an image of strength and confidence to his family because he lacks the opportunity and ability to compete successfully in the white world. In order to maintain some semblance of self-esteem, he offsets these deficiencies by compensation in sexual prowess, irresponsibility, peer interaction, wife beating, and lack of desire to compete.

His behavior reinforces his feelings of inadequacy as a household head and propels him further into a negative stance. Even a job may not solve the problems of the family relationship, once it is established. In one extensive study of placing hard-core unemployed in industry, it was found that in general, rather than easing tension in the home, the new job status for the black man intensified previous tensions and created new problems. These were manifested in the wife's refusal to help the husband get ready for work, her neglect of the house, increasing jealousies, and so forth. The conclusion was that employment for the black man forced the conflict over the matriarchal role to the surface. The man assumed a new economic posture that changed the family structure—the

69

underlying, pervasive assumption of male unreliability was upset. The authors of this study note that there is a large investment in the validity of such a premise, from within the household as well as from outside institutions.[33]

The nature of father-child relationships covers a wide spectrum and consists of a paradoxical element. When the father and child live separately, the usual position of the father is an acknowledgment of his paternity, an admission of financial responsibility (which is acted upon on an irregular basis), and contact with the child on an irregular, infrequent, and short-duration basis. Men not living with their child tend to be more affectionate and tender to the child than those living together, who often give little time and attention to their offspring.[34] That men are often more involved and more affectionate with other men's children might negate, to a certain degree, the statistical implications drawn from divorce rates and absentee figures of child development that is void of paternal contact. It is not to be denied that there is a difference between quality and quantity of a relationship. The point is that while there may be a numerically high absenteeism among biological fathers, the ghetto household, nevertheless, is not totally lacking in masculine influences.[35]

Elliot Liebow's classic book *Talley's Corner*[36] portrays the black ghetto man in his street-corner role. If this portrayal is authentic for a viable percentage of adult males, their lives seem to be characterized by loose and short-term relationships—they are unable to capture the "acceptable" forms of reinforcement and status; therefore, they turn to their peer relationships at the street corner to capture some meaning to their existence. Their role vis-a-vis society is passive, and their self-assessment negative and accepting. It may be significant, however, that a decade has passed since Liebow's research.

Nathan Caplan, in writing about the "New Ghetto Man," characterizes him in somewhat different terms.[37] Caplan finds that he is less satisfied with the kinds of menial, low-paying, low-status jobs that have provided the bulk of employment for the ghetto male (which Liebow's street-corner men submitted to on a regular basis and did not seem to aspire to rise above). This dissatisfaction with being underemployed, coupled with an increasing black consciousness and positive feeling about his race, tend to a rejection of the submissive street-corner posture.

There are, then, alternative male role models available and evident to the black male child. But either is an inadequate model with respect to providing an adaptation device to cope with the values and demands of the larger, dominant culture. The black male is not able to help his child develop responsibility, the prerequisite to a strong job posture. If the ghetto father is newly displaced from the rural South, his job skills are not likely to be applicable to the city. He is unable to teach his child a legitimate means of earning a living. If he is successful in the ghetto setting, it is likely to be in some activity considered antisocial by the larger society. In any case, it is not likely to be a model that builds aspiration for education and normal career success for many ghetto children.

Aside from the parental situation, the entire ghetto structure present the young black male with an enormous handicap: since the middle-class "normal" models are not available, how can they be a part of his developmental process when they do not exist within the sphere of his young world?[38] Very early, when he should be molding a sense of stability, significance, and routine that revolve around a working father, he is, instead, part of a household that lacks a father figure; or, even if there is exposure to a working father, his job may be unrewarding (both monetarily and personally) and provide a negative work image. There seems to be no doubt that this lack of exposure to positive work attitudes is detrimental. The literature seems to be totally in consensus on this point—lower-class black children are deprived of relevant work models in the daily work experiences of parents, relatives, and neighbors, including the casual and informal introduction to the role of the worker and to the "language" of work.

The Ghetto School Experience

The young black ghetto dweller's existence is characterized by ambiguities and the initial shaky stages of a survival system. Armed with this posture, ghetto black children approach school, where their attitudes are often submissive or precociously independent, reflecting their "bad" perception of themselves. There is widespread evidence that the educational experience is far different for the ghetto dweller than it is for the middle-class student.

The controversial question of whether minority children are

deficient in their capabilities for academic achievement is too complex to be dealt with here. However, this issue has been the target of much recent research that seems to be aware of the entire anatomy of the problem—that inequalities in school resources and expenditures and in physical opportunities to study and learn render research that ignore these factors invalid.[39] Myopic conclusions that have been advanced in the past about inadequate abilities and low-level aspirations of minority children have been largely negated through research that considers cultural and social opportunities, home environment, the mental set of the child, as well as nutritional deficiencies, and the fact that the subject is often handicapped by a predetermined labeling process that could affect both the subject and the researcher.[40]

Intensive work done in the Harlem schools showed that teachers become increasingly irrelevant and ineffective to children as they pass through elementary school.[41] Therefore, one potentially viable source of positive reinforcement is eliminated. The influence of the teacher is replaced by that of peers, and motives of these peer groups are generally counter to motives and expectations of the school system, resulting in an atmosphere that is not conducive to academic achievement. If a child is motivated and manages to remain somewhat immune to the nonproductive peer pressure, the ghetto school system is not geared to provide the proper tools and reinforcement to fuel this motivation. Ghetto schools are operated much more along the lines of a holding and maintenance stance than as a source of guidance, basic knowledge, authority, and inspiration.[42]

More than fifteen years ago James B. Conant viewed the neglect of inner-city youth by the school system with respect to preparation and guidance for employment as a severe and tragic situation.[43] The current literature indicates little improvement.

There is no easy way of evaluating the impact of an education system. One study showing figures for the New York public education system is a strong indictment against the system as a vehicle to help the minority youth improve his or her status, or even to provide any kind of equality in educational opportunities.[44] The tracking system, which supposedly segregates students according to ability, is seen as a way of stigmatizing and depriving children and of profoundly affecting their futures. In fact, studies show almost total independence between school grades and the intelligence of those who get them.[45] In 1967 the high school population in the New York system was composed of 40 percent nonwhites (mostly poor), yet only 7 percent of graduates from New York academic high schools who went on to college were black or Puerto Rican.[46] National data show that the black-white gap in educational achievement has shrunk from three years to three months in the past decade.[47] But that data provide no insight as to educational quality or to the conditions in ghetto schools.

Recent census data indicate that graduation from college has become increasingly dependent on one's social-class background.[48] If education is the key to mobility, the public school system may be playing a major role in the self-perpetuating nature of the ghetto environment.

Responses from high school boys to interview questions attempting to determine opportunity structure are revealing (see Table 12). Schools do not seem to do much for the self-esteem and career prospects of many ghetto youth. Undoubtedly, a few with unusual tenacity, ability, or parental or other influence "make it." But the picture painted by the research is of overwhelming obstacles.

The Ghetto Child

The socialization process of the young boy results in a certain life style that is congruent with ghetto acceptance. To gain an understanding of ghetto youths (as a preliminary to understanding their motivation, value systems, attitudes toward work, and so on), one must first develop an appreciation for this life style—the skills, heroes, and priorities that make up its composite parts. "Playing it cool" is a distinctive dimension of the *gestalt* of ghetto youth. Rainwater calls it part of the "expressive life-style," which is the art of making oneself interesting and attractive to others in order better to manipulate their behavior in a way that will provide immediate gratification.[49] Being "cool" incorporates a number of personality items, including a highly specialized medium of verbal communication. The "cool" process is fairly well-defined with respect to clothing, ways of walking, and an admiration for hustlers and pimps, who live well from the efforts of others.[50] It is perceived as being necessary to survival, but its long-run rewards are often

Table 12. Percentage of Boys Answering "True" to Opportunity Structure Questions, by Race, Class, and Gang Status

| | Percent Answering "True" | | | | | |
| | Negro | | | White | | |
Interviewer: "Once again I want you to think about the area where your group hangs out. I'm going to read a few statements to you, and all you have to do is say 'True' or 'False' after each statement. If you think the statement is true about the area, say 'True'; if you don't think it's true, say 'False.'"	Lower class, gang N = 206	Lower class, nongang N = 89	Middle class N = 26	Lower class, gang N = 90	Lower class, nongang N = 79	Middle class N = 53
Legitimate Educational Opportunities						
1. In our area its hard for a young guy to stay in school. (−)*	48.5	28.1	7.7	52.2	21.5	0.0
3. Most of the guys in our area will graduate from high school. (+)	30.6	44.9	96.2	32.3	65.8	100.0
4. In our area, there are a lot of guys who want to go to college. (+)	37.4	47.2	84.6	16.7	44.3	98.1
Criminal Learning Structures						
14. There are connections in this area for a guy who wants to make good money illegally. (+)	57.8	49.4	38.5	47.8	35.4	5.7
15. Young guys can learn a lot about crime from older people in the area. (+)	75.2	66.3	34.6	52.2	35.4	11.3
16. There are adults in this area who help young guys make money illegally. (+)	59.2	49.4	30.8	42.2	26.6	15.1

SOURCE: Nona Glazer and Carol Creedon, eds., *Children and Poverty: Some Sociological and Psychological Perspectives* (Chicago: Rand McNally, 1968), pp. 288–89. The table is a sample, omitting questions 5–13.

*Signs in parentheses indicate the "valence" of a "true" answer, relative to the opportunity structure area indicated.

disappointment and unhappiness because the more a boy is into the "cool" world, the more he has to accept defeat in a society where upward mobility is an admired aspiration.

As the young black male moves through the preadolescent years, parental and school influences diminish and are largely replaced by peer group dominance. Peer group influence in and of itself is not abnormal behavior for young boys. It does, however, pose problems when it displaces more positive influences and becomes the springboard for deviant behavior and frequent encounters with the law. Since there is a marked deficiency in proper socialization through the home environment, peer group activity, hustling, and street savvy fill this role. Ghetto youth gang involvement is more prevalent among boys than girls and fosters stealing, drinking, use of narcotics, fighting, promiscuity, and producing children prior to marriage.[51] Interviews conducted with known drug addicts revealed that the first use of a hard drug was never experienced alone, but was always in the presence, and often under pressure, of peers. The almost inevitable result is a loss of interest in school and work and immersion in crime, including stealing from and conning family and friends. One study identified 60 percent of a group of young addicts to have committed crime before addiction and 96 percent after, 80 percent to have been in school before and 24 percent after.[52]

That such deviant behavior often explodes into violence is readily apparent, but its causes pose a crucial question. The ghetto life itself is rampant with violence—the bite of a rat, an unprovoked beating, a corrupt political machine, and so forth.[53] Extreme violence—murder, rape, and armed robbery—tends to be executed through the gang mechanism.[54] Each member of the gang must prove to every other member his manhood and his lack of fears or consequences. The perverse nature and severe consequences of gang action thus are an extreme part of the inherent violence of the ghetto.

Gang participation is not universal. The literature reveals a variety of roles acted out by various ghetto youth—the gouster, the ivy leaguer, the hustler, the conservative, and the mockman, according to one source,[55] the stoic, the defeated, the exploiter, the achiever, the rebel, the activist, and the revolutionary, according to another.[56] But that the image which exalts the male youth with his peers is one that precludes successful employment in the jobs available seems to be a consensus of the research.[57] The evidence does not support a view of deficiency in intelligence or competence. In fact, it portrays a remarkable adaptability and well-developed survival skills, but skills that are not applied to success in employment.

The portrayal of the female child of the ghetto differs sharply from that of the male. Parents appear to make a greater effort to provide motivation, higher expectation, and upward yearning.[58] But those yearnings are likely to be doused by early pregnancy and submersion in the pattern of welfare-supported female family head. The girl is described also as beginning with idealistic dreams of the man she will marry but succumbing to a realistic disillusionment at about sixteen to eighteen years of age. "Perhaps it is their understanding of the role that racist society plays in keeping the male in a perpetual state of subordination that causes them not to dream and hope for the right kind of boyfriend who, to them, does not exist."[59]

Employment for Ghetto Inhabitants

The approach to the labor market significantly dichotomizes the respective positions of ghetto and of middle-class youths. In this arena the black youth's deprivation—in regard to education, race, social class, lack of proper role models—severely handicaps him or her. It is important to distinguish between a *lack* of skills—knowledge, desire, personality, and ability—and the *application* of these traits that are relevant to job performance. Cultural deprivation, in the form of functional illiteracy, a lack of basic education and social graces, inadequacies in math and science, and judgmental deficiency, are revealed when young blacks enter the labor market. From an assessment of his or her ability to acquire and hold a job, it could be concluded that this cultural deprivation is not offset by the fact that these young people possess many of the traits that are deemed desirable by middle-class standards: courage, leadership, ingenuity, tenacity, intelligence, ability to manage people, and highly developed verbal skills.[60]

Unlike his lower-class white cohort, the black male youth has not acquired the routine socialization that allows him to identify with factory and office work. Poor posture, nonstandard language, radical grooming, health problems, insecurity, and lack of self-confidence in unfamiliar surroundings are all obstacles to employment.[61] The fact that he possesses highly developed skills—skills that have enabled him not only to survive but to be viewed as highly successful within the ghetto—does not mean that these talents are transferrable to the arena of employment. A highly skilled street youth experiences a marked loss of self-esteem when he is inadequate on a job. He reestablishes his self-esteem by quitting the job and returning to the familiar setting of the street, where his competencies are appreciated as assets. Recognition of this concept of competing competencies (ghetto versus employment competency states) helps to explain the failure of training programs for ghetto youths.[62] These sociopsychological aspects are reinforced by the stark economic realities stressed in Chapter 3. The legal ghetto economy is mostly composed of low-asset, low-profit, nondurable manufacturing and small retail trades that create an atmosphere of oppression and discouragement of the ghetto youth. Evidence is strong that the poor want to work,[63] but not that their desire is realistic in terms of the alternatives.

In contrast to the paucity of positive job-oriented models for the young ghetto dweller to emulate, there is an abundance of negative role models. The entertainer and the athlete are admired, but the routes of access to these occupations are not open and apparent.[64] The young black male is more frequently exposed to the seemingly rewarding life of the hustler, who ostensibly displays the monetary rewards of his profession. A major part of the hustler's profile is spending money on expensive, flashy cars, clothing, and jewelry. The hustling ethic is expressed mainly as an obsessive drive to become wealthy and display such wealth and an extreme contempt for work, especially the type available to lower-class blacks. It is difficult to estimate the number of hustlers as a percentage of the ghetto population; but the hustler displays himself much more prominently (that is part of his makeup)—his "success" is much more evident than that of the worker. Julius Hudson states, "Virtually all lower class black male youth hang out in pool rooms at one time or another."[65] Thus they are exposed to the pool hustler at the very least, and most likely to those engaged in the more lucrative illegal activities—the sale of sex and narcotics.

While there is an element of risk involved in the sale of drugs, it is the most lucrative and consistent activity. The life of the pimp offers far less risk, more glamor, and a high payoff, but it requires rather narrowly defined personality components. Pool hustling and running numbers have a lower rating on the reward and status scale, but they also have less risk. As Table 12 suggests, these appear to be highly available and consistent methods of earning money. Some authors see successful participation in this "sporting life" as a manifestation, given the opportunities available, of the same entrepreneurship and spirit of free enterprise that is admired in the businessman of the broader society.[66]

Louis Ferman at the University of Michigan has assembled a massive compilation of interviews with ghetto hustlers of various specialties. Students from indigeneous backgrounds have interviewed at length pimps, prostitutes, numbers runners, and dope peddlers in Detroit and obtained amazingly frank biographies of their life styles, earnings, and techniques. The returns are portrayed as very high for the successful.[67] Those interviewed clearly assessed the risks and returns to various illicit enterprises, portraying a businesslike attitude to the endeavors.

Paul Bullock writes that many academicians indicate their distance from reality by the lack of attention they give to the economic significance of illegal markets, which encompass the production, sale, and consumption of hard and soft drugs, gambling, illegal betting, prostitution, and pimping. "Rather than being marginal or of uncertain importance, the subeconomy is probably the greatest single source of market income for young men in the central city.[68] How much can be earned from such sources is subject only to speculation. Some articles mention figures as high as $75,000 to $100,000 per year.[69] As noted above, however, it is probably not the amount earned but the conspicious rewards in comparison to the alternatives available that is the attraction. Since the possibility and even probability of jail is something many grow up with, it has already been discounted as a cost and a deterrent.[70]

The lucrative payoff, the glamor aspect, and the minimal risk of illegal activities are in marked contrast to the relatively non-lucrative, degrading, disappointing, and scarce aspects of legal employment. An explicit account of this contrast can be gained from the reply given by a gang warlord when asked why he did not go downtown to get a job. "I make $40 or $50 a day selling marijuana. You want me to go down to the garment district and push one of those trucks through the streets and at the end of the week take home $40 to $50 if I'm lucky?"[71]

The 1971 *Manpower Report of the President* provides a vivid description:

> The absence of employment opportunities which could lead to a radical improvement in life styles and movement out of the slums seemed to be the basic reason why jobs, even those which pay above the minimum wage, were sometimes regarded disdainfully. The young people interviewed had little hope of significant increases in earnings, because they saw so little chance of an occupational breakthrough. At best, they expected marginal employment at wages which would allow them to "get by." The incentive to work hard in order to effect a major change in their way of life was absent.
>
> Hustling was often regarded as a logical and rational option. The market for gambling, numbers, prostitution, and narcotics is large and highly profitable, and the possibility of "being on one's own" competes powerfully with the opportunities available in the regulated middle-class world.
>
> Criminal activities and the possible handicap of an arrest record did not seem to present problems for these Harlem youth. Issues of this kind were not even raised during the interviews. This finding suggests that the costs attached to engaging in illegal activities tend to be low. No great social stigma accompanies arrest, so far as the immediate neighborhood is concerned. Job opportunities are already limited by other barriers, so that the effect of an arrest record is not considered important. The probability of being apprehended is considered relatively small. And the penalty for a particular offense, if one is caught, can be calculated with reasonable accuracy. Thus, an individual engaged in hustling is usually aware of the chance he is taking.

A surprise also lurks in the description from this source:

> To gage the impact of illegal activities on the participation of slum residents in the regular labor market, the unemployment rates for workers in the slums of 16 cities in 1966 were correlated with crime rates in these cities. Unemployment was found to be lowest in the cities with the greatest amount of property crime. It appears that the larger the sources of illegal income, the fewer the people in the slums who persist in looking for legitimate jobs (or the greater the numbers who report themselves as employed when they are not, in order to explain their style of life to the enumerators).[72]

The severity of the situation then emerges. A more or less consistent theme running through the literature is that young people in the slums are acutely aware of a system that seems to offer rewards to those who illegally exploit others and does not reward those who struggle under the traditional methods. The rational choices appear to be shunning work to adopt exploitation and hustling, totally turning off via drugs, and foregoing marriage in favor of more casual, temporary alliances. The pattern seems to reinforce itself from generation to generation. The resourcefulness, initiative, and presence of a value structure manifested by young black ghetto dwellers cannot be denied. The problem lies in the channeling mechanism for these positive attributes.

Behavior that labels the ghetto youth as deviant is not perceived by him as a mark of shame, but is part of the process of rejection of the white middle-class value system that eludes slum boys because of their color and their perceptions of opportunity. This psychology is spelled out explicitly by Michael Schwartz and George Henderson. [73] They ask what happens when a value system congruent with hard work is perceived as unrealistic because of a closed opportunity structure and chronic unemployment. The answer is that a dissonant situation emerges. This conflict is resolved by restructuring the value system—work is devalued as a means of obtaining money and other means are substituted.

A large percentage of ghetto youth remain, however, who are unable to resolve personal conflict this way. Their situation is also a dissonant one—they are aware of the standards and values of the larger society, but feel inadequate and ill equipped to fit in. They live out their lives in a helpless limbo. They neither succumb totally nor are able to escape.

The Result: A Dysfunctional Life Style

The negligible effect on unemployment as a result of the vast amount of time, money, and effort expended on employment and training programs is indicative of the absence of any single, fast, easy solution. The ghetto adolescent is the product of history and society; what can be offered as a solution to his or her problems is illusive. The solution, undoubtedly, is tied to understanding the complex ghetto youth and the ghetto environment. Is the problem deeply embedded in the family structure, as Moynihan accuses? To what extent is that structure a product of outside institutions? Is the ghetto youth unemployed because of a lack of desire to be employed or because there is no job for him or her?

The contrast is clearly drawn in the literature. In the normal process of human development and socialization, children are exposed to the work values of parents who work in paid employment or in the home, who consider work necessary and important and often satisfying and fulfilling. They soon become aware of the role that work plays in society and in their own lives. In the process of exploring themselves, they fantasize themselves in various work roles and gradually adopt the standard American view that one is what he or she does. They learn to make decisions, become aware of alternatives, make tentative choices, and undergo a preparation process.

The nonghetto youth, with his background of exposure to the routine and importance of work, can use this exposure and the experiences he has accumulated as a framework on which to build and develop his own personal path of career development. As they reach working age, middle-class young people tend to go through three major stages, or attitudinal sets, as they become immersed in the labor market.[74] The first of these stages is referred to as a moratorium period and is characterized mainly by participation in the labor market on an occasional basis. Work is not the primary concern; usually the educational process they are still involved in is more important. Advancement from this stage is to the exploration stage—different jobs are tried and discarded while the groundwork is laid for a long-term job commitment. At the conclusion of a fruitful exploration period, the person arrives at the settling-down stage—a kind of work is chosen and a job secured while more solid thought is given to the future. Not every young person goes through this process, but the demand of career education is in this direction. This is essentially the prevailing model.

This rather definitive process may be a luxury the ghetto young cannot afford because of their immediate needs and low-income status. Additionally, they often do not possess the necessary framework, the background characteristics, personal network, and opportunities that enable them to follow this general pattern. The picture that emerges from the literature of growing up in the ghetto is in sharp contrast to that of middle-class youth.

Too many in the ghetto have no working role model in the home, at least not one who has an admirable job or who enjoys and excels at homemaking. The work values and attitudes toward work may be negative. More likely the problem will be that desirable work roles will never be perceived as a reality.

At the awareness stage, the awareness is likely to be that hard work has few rewards, that illicit activity and corruption may pay better, and that one is not a part of the predominant society and has no obligation to it. A rational exploration of one's capabilities and preferred life style as contrasted to one's opportunities may justify a deviant approach to achieving universally desired ends. The most able may choose to apply their entrepreneurial skills to the opportunities that appear most obvious and most rewarding.

Liebow and Caplan portray alternative accommodations to the circumstances and perhaps indicate trends. Liebow's street-corner man has been defeated by life and has resigned.[75] Caplan's "new ghetto man" has developed the skills of survival and put them to work to gain within his environment the rewards all put first.[76] Beyond simple brute survival, all seek a sense of self-worth, usually reflected in one's perception of peer opinion. Only a unique few in that setting survive the perverse influence of home, neighborhood, school, and alternative income opportunities to achieve success in the terms dictated by the alien society outside the ghetto.

Claude Brown in his autobiographical *Manchild in the Promised Land*[77] and Malcolm X in his autobiography[78] portray well the rigors of that trek. More typical is the labor market analysis inadvertently provided by Brown in his *Children of Ham*.[79] Harlem youth, boys and girls, leave the untenable environment of homes shattered by unemployment, poverty, drink, drugs, and strife. They personally have experienced prostitution, drug addiction, and other ills, and have rejected them. They set up housekeeping as a teenage family in an abandoned tenement. Faced with economic reality, they adapt to the opportunities available. One serves as mother and homemaker. One runs numbers. Another delivers bootleg booze. Another steals, on order, clothes of prescribed size and style, appliances, or anything else his customers want. They refuse to become involved in the hard drug traffic, which they detest. Only one has a job that would count him as employed in the Current Population Survey. They adapt to the environment and and survive with admirable ingenuity. And who is to fault them?

5

Conclusions and Recommendations

The general causes of ghetto youth unemployment are starkly clear from the literature, though many details remain to be filled in: (1) *perverse demographic trends*, releasing from the central cities those most capable of adaptation to the broader society and incarcerating within the ghetto the least experienced and the oldest, the failures, and the accumulated victims of past discrimination; (2) *deteriorating economies*, steadily drained of those economic opportunities that have traditionally been the critical bottom rungs of the mobility ladder for generations of youth and immigrants; (3) *dysfunctional life styles*, in which success produces failure because street wisdom and the requisites of peer acceptance are precisely the attributes that militate against employment and career progress. These have all been adequately documented in previous chapters. Only their implications need to be treated here.

An examination of their intensity and magnitude characterizes as palliatives all that has been attempted in public policy solutions. That is not to know emergency first aid. If the victim is bleeding, grab the tourniquet but don't mistake it for a suture. Lasting solutions must attack real causes. How can central city populations be decentralized and exposed to attractive employment opportunity? How can the central city economy be redeveloped? How can crime be made to pay less than employment? How can the ghetto life style be modified in relation to its career development consequences?

No easy answers emerge, but perhaps some useful insights do. One is a time dimension. The central city phenomenon is a consequence of decades of policy and nonpolicy. Agricultural policies as well as income differentials drove former sharecroppers and tenant farmers cityward four decades ago. A federal housing program subsidized a massive movement of white semiskilled, craft and technical workers to the suburbs three decades ago. A federal highway program two decades ago made intercity transportation easy and intracity movement difficult. School systems over thirty years have reflected the demands of their taxpaying patrons rather than the needs of their students. None of these policies will be reversed quickly. Solutions must be long-term ones over generations, not tied to the next election. The family plays a critical role. Whether it is weak or strong in the context of survival in the ghetto circumstances, it does not give sound career development signals. There is likely to be no real solution that does not rebuild the family's influence or create a substitute for it. But who knows how to do that?

Population distribution versus central city economic development is a limited choice. Manufacturing plants and their satellites are not going to return to the central city. Either the ghetto young must be prepared for those desirable jobs that exist in the central city, or they must be encouraged or enabled to move to the suburbs more rapidly. That does not mean there is no place for low-level jobs as long as they are way stations rather than final destinations in a working career to which there are other income alternatives. Outmigration from the ghetto might be accelerated by scattering public and subsidized housing about the suburban landscape. Enlistment in the military or enrollment in such programs as the Job Corps and the Young Adult Conservation Corps might be used to acclimate the young and to place them in suburban settings.

Job Corps already has ties with unions but could be tied in better with the schools and the military. School credit could be earned in a Job Corps setting, preliminary to transition to regular school enrollment for some. The equivalent of "Coop" programs in vocational education might take central city youth into suburban or metropolitan settings, house them in Job Corps centers, provide part-time training interspersed with related employment under Job Corps staff supervisors and ease their transition to full-time employment in a new residential setting. The Job Corps should be an excellent facility for preparing such youth to pass military entrance requirements. The military itself over time has been one of the most potent institutions in generating geographical relocation. Many of the youth of concern are now rejected by the military services, which may find it necessary to repeat something like its Project 100,000 to save the volunteer armed forces. Those just under the acceptable requirements were recruited and functioned well, though never to the satisfaction of a military establishment accustomed to the manpower "fat" of a conscription system.[1] Urban renewal, which has been described as Negro removal, may be desirable if sufficient attention is given to the landing place.

Too little is known about the number and nature of the central city jobs that lie between the white-collar and professional ones with high education requirements, the disappearing semiskilled operative jobs, and the unattractive jobs that are readily spurned. Many highly respected jobs in municipal government without elevated education requirements are still held by commuting suburban residents. The San Francisco post office a few years ago recruited youth who could not pass civil service entrance exams into temporary jobs, where they were trained and coached to achieve permanent placement.[2] They turned out to be better than average employees, but the project, beyond some lip service, was never incorporated elsewhere.

Every city has its variety of skilled jobs and the more attractive among semiskilled ones, if they can be identified and preparation for and access to them provided. Subsidized apprenticeships in building service, automotive mechanics, and distributive jobs might provide the necessary incentives to both employers and youth in areas where catch-as-catch-can learning has been the prevailing mode. With all of the debate about assuring a white-black mix in the schools, it is probably true that sufficient resources (and not just money) addressed to the urban schools could prepare substantial numbers to compete for white-collar and the more attractive service jobs. It has been too soon forgotten that the institutional and on-the-job training programs of the Manpower Development and Training Act did lead to substantial gains for youth when tied directly to available employment opportunities.[3]

Public service employment as a structural weapon rather than a general countercyclical tool would allocate more of its slots to the central city and provide controllable opportunities for both youth and their parents. The special project approach of the 1976 Comprehensive Employment and Training Act (CETA) amendments may be the wrong emphasis in this regard. For dignity, it is necessary that there be as few distinguishing marks as possible between CETA jobs and the regular civil service. Since the annual average number of unemployed central city youth was only 535,000 in 1976, reallocation of even a small portion of the current 750,000 CETA public service employment slots could have a major impact. Yet at present only one-fifth of such slots are reaching any youth. The Youth Employment and Demonstration Projects Act (YEDPA) may generate as much as one-third of the required temporary employment opportunities, but it is not limited to the target group of locations. The Local Public Works Program allocated to the maximum extent to central cities could provide respected and well-paid construction jobs and refurbish a deteriorating environment, if accompanied by a persistent apprenticeship outreach effort. A number of cities, notably Baltimore, are having good results from enriched work-experience programs when linked with basic education and on-the-job training.[4] In any case, to be useful, the jobs must be real, demand performance, and have the potential for transition to lasting and unsubsidized employment. Dignity and positive career development in the central city family may depend as much on the source of income as on the alleviation of poverty.

All of these solutions are prosaic in comparison to the intensity of the problem. Redeveloping or breaking up the ghetto and rebuilding the family is the logical policy implication flowing from the facts. But no one seems to have a practical prescription for that set of maladies.

An Agenda for Further Research on Ghetto Youth Unemployment

Urban youth unemployment is a problem with many dimensions and one that cuts across a number of disciplinary lines, including economics, sociology, and psychology. The absolute magnitudes and relative proportions of the unemployment dilemma for urban youth are becoming increasingly well documented by a number of government data sources. The underlying causes and factors have been partially identified in much of the literature cited in this survey, but more research should be focused on the problem if public policy is to be effective in dealing with the issue. The following agenda identifies and discusses areas in which further research is needed.

The Ghetto Economy

The economic structure of the ghetto and surrounding central city still harbors many mysteries. A great deal of work needs to be done to clarify the nature of those ghetto economies and their relationships to the broader economy.

1. Our earlier discussion dealt with the ghetto economy in highly aggregated terms, suggesting that a relationship exists between the slowing patterns of employment growth in all central cities combined and urban youth unemployment rates during the 1970s. There is no reason to assume that such a relationship is true for all cities in the nation. In fact, the usual assumption is that the impact of stagnant employment growth on youth unemployment rates is greater in the older, mature cities located in the Northeast and Midwest industrial belt. A disaggregation of employment change during the 1970s for the larger SMSAs, as well as information on the number and shares of unemployed and out-of-work teenagers, both total and by race, in these cities would be valuable. Current data show that 60 percent of all unemployed black teenagers are located in the central city; identification of the specific cities that have the heaviest concentration of this group would be important. There is an additional need to identify these city-specific unemployed teen groups in terms of those who are both out of school and out of work. Any significant intercity variation in this measure might reveal which cities are more heavily impacted by teenage groups who do not consider either school or work as their major activity. A sample set of such hard-core cities could be analyzed on a comparative basis with other cities that do not experience high levels of youth alienation from both the education system and the labor force.

2. Youth unemployment rates in the central city are persistently higher than in the surrounding suburbs, and recent data suggest that overall black employment in cities has not been responsive to the moderate recovery within the national economy. While unemployment rates decreased between 1975 and 1976 in nineteen of the largest metropolitan areas, gains for black workers were apparent in only eleven of these areas. Geographic differences in un-

employment rates and significantly varying capabilities of urban economies to recover seem to be permanent. A second research need is for a more detailed analysis of the city and ghetto economic structure, particularly in terms of its susceptibility to cyclical fluctuations in comparison to its long-run secular performance as an employer of the total and the youth labor forces. The spatial propagation of national fluctuations through our urban system may differentially affect youth as well as overall unemployment rates if the geographic pattern of this propagation is uneven, as suggested by David Jeffrey.[5] This in turn would entail an analysis of factors that might contribute to a greater vulnerability of some city and ghetto economies to the business cycle. These two research needs could be met by standard statistical agencies using straight-forward establishment data but with a greater wealth of detail.

3. More intensive case studies are needed of the types of firms and industries and their occupations that comprise the urban labor market for youths. One might speculate that some ghetto economies are composed of marginally productive firms using antiquated capital equipment and a traditional vertical production flow. An export sector or base approach would be one initial framework in which to examine and measure some aspects of this industrial structure. Youth and adult ghetto employment would be dis-aggregated into production activities for the local, domestic economy and into employment-production activities for the external, non-ghetto economy. The share of ghetto employment represented by the export sector can offer some clues to the problem of cyclical instability and insights into the economic constraints operating on central city employment change. What is the competitive structure of those industries and how do the firms in them survive? Do successful firms employ ghetto youth? What are the characteristics of those firms and of the youth they employ? Only case studies of statistically representative firms can answer these questions.

The possible implications for the stability of youth unemployment as well as wage rates paid to teenagers should be studied more carefully and might very well be modeled along the lines of Oster-mann's work,[6] which emphasizes the importance of bridge jobs for urban teenagers as they make the transition from school to work. Little is known about employment by occupation by age in central cities. It is a general assumption that only low-paid, unattractive jobs and those requiring substantial education and "polish" exist there. But no economy can survive without a middle layer of semi-skilled and skilled blue-collar jobs. What and how many are they, who gets them, and what are the access routes for youth?

4. The irregular (or illicit) economy needs more investigation, perhaps within the context of a high-growth employment sector that offers superior earnings and employment opportunities over the conventional sector. Its nature prohibits investigation by government statistical agencies. Instead, intensive, in-depth interviews will have to be undertaken by indigenous interviewers in sufficient cities in various parts of the country to account for significant regional or city size differences. Sociologist Louis Ferman, as noted in Chapter 4, has accumulated a vast quantity of such interviews for Detroit.[7] They reflect amazing candor, but the queries are sociological in emphasis. Equal emphasis should be given to the economics of the ghetto scene. What proportion of a ghetto population can make a living by irregular and illicit means? How do the average levels of earnings by activity compare to those in the legitimate sector? Who are the customers? To what extent is it an export industry bringing in incomes from outside the ghetto as contrasted with exploiting other ghetto residents? To what extent do the activities represent careers as opposed to sporadic and part-time involvement? What are the mobility patterns between legal and illicit activities? What special set of talents and skills are needed for success in the irregular economy and how do they relate to the skills required by the regular economy? The questions are many; the technique is crucial.

Most observers agree that crime, hustling, and irregular activities in general offer viable alternatives to regular ghetto employment—yet many of these observations are based on casual observation or on tentative dollar estimates of the magnitude of activity in this type of illicit, urban sector. There is also some reason to suspect that discouraged workers and dropouts in the ghetto in fact find employment in this sector. All these factors have a direct implication for labor force participation. Ferman's work suggests that decision to enter the irregular employment sector is not a capricious decision by youth, but one that is subject not only to peer group pressure but also to more tangible constraints such as job availability and earnings in the legitimate sector. This type of research at the micro level—that is, within a limited number of ghettos and for a small yet statistically relevant sample size—needs to be extended in order to identify the irregular type of employment in terms of opportunity costs, expected earnings, and risk. Such a research effort can be formulated in terms of an expected payoff calculus adjusted by the risk of apprehension and the risk (one suspects low in many situations) of conviction.

Teenage Unemployment and Job Search Behavior

Job-search behavior raises a number of research issues related to urban labor markets and ghetto youths.

1. The transition from school to work involves a job-search process by teenagers that may be qualitatively different for ghetto youth. Stanley P. Stephenson[8] has examined some aspects of youth job-search behavior for white and black teenagers, using 1971 data for Indianapolis. The nature of this process for ghetto youths needs to be studied, particularly in view of our earlier discussion on dysfunctional life styles that may be a factor unique to ghetto teenagers. This job-search analysis should be designed to include the nature of information flows within the ghetto job market, as well as the cognitive ability of individuals to perceive different employment and career opportunities. Expected wages and job stability characteristics should be part of a study on youth job search. An example of such data is the special May 1976 survey of three thousand unemployed persons cited by Julius Shiskin[9] that discovered that about half of the unemployed willing to accept jobs at $2.30 an hour were teenagers. This kind of expectation behavior by the young needs to be examined within the context of central city and ghetto environments. What information do ghetto teenagers have as they begin job search? How accurate and complete is it? How do they in fact find jobs, and how does this differ from the job-search methods used by suburban youth? Are jobs of higher quality available which they could fill but cannot or do not find access to? Time and again job-search studies have shown the informal assistance of successful relations and friends to be the key element. What, if anything, is substituted if this support is lacking? Or is this phenomenon a major factor in attracting youth to illicit activities as the major outlet to which they can be guided by successful friends? Job-search studies can be accomplished only by querying large numbers of young people to find out what they know and what they do in job search.

2. Studies by Levitan and Taggart,[10] Peter Doeringer and Michael Piore,[11] and others have identified teenagers as peripheral workers, usually in secondary, low-skill, low-paying jobs that represent unstable employment opportunities. This type of employment is typically characterized by high turnover with teenagers frequently out of work, between jobs, and more generally experiencing a transition from these secondary jobs to more meaningful employment as they exit from school and explore longer-term labor market possibilities. The nature of the search process is critical in terms of the resources and information youth can rely on in place of harsh experience and labor market failure.

A systematic survey of labor market information mechanisms and the accessibility to jobs within the larger metropolitan labor market needs to be conducted for selected central cities, especially those with traditionally high teenage jobless rates. Such a survey would identify the availability and accessibility of public school counseling, public employment service agencies, and other non-government information services. This kind of research effort would offer a preliminary basis from which further research design could depart. In particular, if one can get a feel for the nature of the job-search process by ghetto teens, then one can go on to determine the degree of spatial segmentation and isolation of the central city labor market from the metropolitan economy. Identification of ghetto youth labor immobility in this context would provide one more measure of the extent to which the ghetto is a socioeconomic enclave, cut off from employment opportunities in the larger urban surroundings.

Ghetto Youth Unemployment and Later Labor Market Experiences

The consequences of unemployment during the teen years of ghetto youth need to be clearly established. Recent evidence from a study by Avril V. Adams, Garth L. Mangum, et al.[12] suggests that a period of unemployment during the teenage years results in lower earnings and less stable employment in later labor market experiences after controlling for education, socioeconomic status, race, age, and sex. This evidence is based on longitudinal data for a national sample of white and black teenagers and does not include a breakdown for central city or ghetto areas. But it is precisely in these geographic areas that the longer-term labor market consequences of high youth unemployment may be the greatest. A lack of job opportunities may prevent ghetto teenagers from acquiring work skills and knowledge about the world of work, experiences that affect their attitudes and longer-term adjustments to the labor market as adult workers. In short, the unemployed ghetto youth of today may become the hard-core unemployed adult worker in the future.

Any analysis of these effects would necessarily entail a longitudinal study on ghetto youth. The National Longitudinal Study sample of black and white teenagers is relevant only to the extent that some similarity is assumed to exist between the nation's urban youth and ghetto teens. Such a highly restrictive assumption leads to the alternatives of (1) analyzing longer-term labor market effects from cross-section data, or (2) the more desirable alternative of developing a longitudinal data series on ghetto workers. Data from the supported work program is one possible point of departure for a longitudinal study.[13] That demonstration project contains employment and earnings data for urban youth on both an experimental and a control basis. The sample size is small and restricted to out-of-school youth, however, and the follow-up is currently designed for only a three year period. A systematic longitudinal analysis of unemployment effects on all categories of ghetto youth could build from the supported work research effort, although the scope of that data source would have to be increased in terms of sample size and time period covered.

Occupation, Education, and Earnings

1. Our earlier discussion touched on the occupation and industry mix of employed teenagers, an aspect that merits further disaggregation into individual cities and, when possible, ghetto areas. This would entail an identification of the kinds of jobs that are available to ghetto youths as they enter the labor force and later as young adults. Duane E. Leigh[14] has studied some aspects of occupational mobility of young men, while Robert E. Hall and Richard Kasten[15] have looked at the broader dimension of economic success. Similar research needs to be carried out for ghetto youths in order to identify any differences between their experiences and environment and that of other metropolitan teenagers. This would neces-

sarily entail some of our earlier discussion on life styles and perhaps the work by Mary Corcoran, Christopher Jencks, and Michael Olnech[16] on family background and economic success.

2. Another important area is the connection between central city education and job skill requirements imposed by urban labor markets on ghetto teenagers and young adults. Much of the existing literature assumes a mismatch between the skill requirements and entry-level jobs for urban youths. Harrison[17] and others have examined this issue for urban workers in general and find it to be a highly overrated proposition. Similar research for ghetto youths is needed in order to determine if they are at a net disadvantage compared with teenagers in the surrounding city and in the suburban ring. Detailed studies would need to probe the entry requirements being imposed by central city employers and compare them to the objective requirements to do the job. The characteristics, geographical origins, microeconomic status, and abilities of those being hired by central city employers would have to be identified and compared to the abilities and preparation of unemployed and sporadically employed ghetto youth. Do the ghetto youth not have the characteristics required by the jobs, or do the employers demand excessive or irrelevent characteristics? What really stands in the way of a match?

3. The opportunity structure of central city neighborhoods and the response of youth to it needs intensive probing. Most cities have available free or at minimum cost an extensive variety of education and training opportunities specifically designed for persons who are out of school or having problems with the regular schools. One might visualize a series of descending concentric circles: (a) the entire youth population; (b) those achieving within the standard education and job structure; (c) those not, but taking advantage of the readily available remedial means; (d) those ignoring such help but accepting enrollment in programs that pay participants; (e) those either ignoring all help, unaware of it, or unable to attain access. Yet these opportunities differ widely from city to city. What is available? Who uses it and who does not? Why not? What are the attractive incentives?

Similarly, though reasonably attractive jobs are scarce in such settings, they do exist and apparently to a greater extent than they are taken advantage of. What is the supply of such jobs? Who gets them? Who ignores them? Why? Do they know of them, do not want them, cannot get access to them, or can they not perform adequately to obtain or keep them?

4. This research leads back to the earlier discussion on identifying the chacteristics and the activities of ghetto teenagers who are not in school or in the labor force. We have some evidence of these relationships for a national sample of teenagers in terms of their pattern of school retention over the business cycle. [18] This framework should be extended to include inner-city and ghetto youths; such an extension might profit by a comparative analysis of the British experience with school leavers and their unemployment problems as reported by A. J. H. Dean. [19]

5. Many of the foregoing issues and needs have been partially fulfilled for national samples of black and white teenagers and need to be explored for ghetto youth. Any research effort that goes in this direction should include the Hispanic youth population, since this is a growing minority group within central cities, and very little literature exists on their employment problems. There are a limited number of reports, such as *The New York Puerto Rican: Patterns of Work Experience*, put out by the New York Bureau of Labor Statistics office, [20] which would be an appropriate starting point for research in this area.

6. The welfare and income consequences of ghetto youth unemployment is another major area of research need. Study for this monograph was not able to unearth any work or measure that related teenagers' contributions to family income. One might be tempted to discount the significance of this in view of the teenagers' tendency to work for pin money and the possibility of welfare as an alternative source of income. But one must also deal with the increasing trend toward female heads of families in central cities, particularly among the black population. Teenage employment may significantly reduce the family income burdens of the female family head.

7. This leads to more complex considerations dealing with teenage earnings, family income, and eligibility for welfare programs. No studies could be uncovered that examined youth employment and unemployment patterns by source and level of family income. Further research in this area should analyze these trade-offs in the context of teenage unemployment and ghetto youth labor force participation.

Minimum Wages and Other Market Impediments

1. A number of studies have established a connection between minimum wage laws and youth unemployment. It would be useful to extend these results specifically to ghetto youth and estimate the wage bill necessary to provide employment to all young persons who seek jobs at the minimum wage. Part of such a study would entail an identification of those central city youth who are searching for jobs and are willing to work below the minimum wage.

2. The importance of other barriers to employment that are also sources of wage rigidities should be examined. One immediately thinks of the credentials gap discussed earlier, a measure of inequality and discrimination that needs to be updated for the 1970s. Other impediments to employment such as apprenticeship, union requirements, and licensing requirements should be identified and the youth unemployment costs should be quantified. A select sample of central cities—both those that are heavily unionized and those that are not—would be a tractable data base for such an analysis. This type of research effort would most likely involve gathering data through appropriate state and local employment agencies. That data should be examined for intercity variations in the unemployment costs of such restrictions and should clearly distinguish impediments and barriers that are not based on job requirements but are based on age and race.

Evolution of the Ghetto Neighborhood, Family, Social Status, Crime, and Deliquency

1. Virtually all of the existing literature on the urban ghetto deals with social-economic characteristics on a cross-section basis. The evolution and life cycle of ghetto economies and neighborhoods is largely a mystery because of the lack of time-series data. The permanency and irreversibility of the ghetto environment and its effect on teenage employment can be dealt with only from the longer view of evolution. Issues such as a separate, dysfunctional life style and a spatially isolated enclave cut off from the mainstream of urban society are other aspects of this longer view. A limited number of studies such as D. P. Slesinger's work[21] on occupation and land use changes in one central city and Harold M. Rose's study[22] of black residential subsystems represent steps in this direction.

2. This approach is especially necessary for any research effort that focuses on the connections between ghetto youth, unemployment, crime as an alternative, and the very elusive yet critical subject of the irregular economy cited above. R. A. Cloward and L. E. Ohlin[23] have argued in terms of a disparity between meager legitimate opportunities and a relative abundance of more attractive, illegitimate opportunities for ghetto teenagers. This distinction in the presence of high inner-city youth unemployment is a mandate for research efforts that can empirically define the dimensions of the problem. Crime and the irregular economy can be analyzed from the more conventional perspective of job opportunities and alternative sources of employment and earnings. This should be extended to include the role of violence, street gang activity, and the drug culture as reported in more popular sources such as Jon Bradshaw.[24] The drug culture seems to offer a considerable abundance of illegal opportunities. It represents a mode of dropping out, an economic source of earnings and employment, and a strong motivating basis for crimes of violence. Does that violence have economic significance? Is it a totally sociological and psychological lashing out at overwhelming personal frustrations? Is it a search for peer acceptance that could be channeled into more acceptable activities?

3. What is the role of law enforcement? What kind of law enforcement, if any, appears to redirect the payoff and incentives to crime as an income source? Can law enforcement policies in different cities be compared to see if a connection exists between effective crime prevention, punishment, role of law enforcers, and other related factors and the relative attractiveness of employment and crime as alternatives?

4. There is also a demographic element in the ghetto youth unemployment-crime matrix that needs to be explored in more detail. The postwar baby boom directly impacted the supply side of urban labor markets by creating larger numbers of teenagers. Another frequently overlooked impact was the changing age structure of urban populations and the incidence of crime. Ongoing research by Allen M. Cole and Charles W. Turner[25] suggests that the expanding population following World War II has intensified competition for social resources such as legitimate jobs. They estimate the "age structure of risk" for various crimes (for example, vandalism occurs primarily between the ages of fourteen and six-

teen, while homicide occurs primarily between the ages of eighteen and twenty-four. Cole and Turner argue that it is possible to explain changes in the age-specific annual rates of social problems (such as criminal arrests for urban and ghetto youths) by the expanding and contracting numbers of people in the high-risk age groups. The declining national birth rate in the years 1962 to 1974 leads to the prediction of a lessening pressure on social resources for young people and a concomitant reduction in criminal activity (for example, this model predicts a 50 percent decline in property crimes between 1975 and 1988). The reduced pressure for sixteen-year-olds should begin in 1978. Although competition for legitimate resources may decline on a national scale, pressure on the ghetto economy may or may not decline. This approach suggests a different research perspective on the problem of youth unemployment, the ghetto environment, and crime.

5. The ghetto family has been the object of considerable research, but sociologists and economists have not cooperated with each other. More intensive work will need to be done on the longitudinal relationships between family life and employment experience. Family life must also be related to migratory patterns. Is it the unsuccessful or the successful family that migrates to the central city or ends up in the ghetto? Does personal and family success diminish the ghetto society? Is it true that the family that becomes economically successful immediately moves to the suburbs, leaving behind only a residue of failures? If so, can the ghetto environment ever improve? What are the characteristics and developments that make possible that move to the suburbs and how do those families fare when they arrive there? Only by identifying those who have moved and then tracing them back along their paths can we answer such questions.

6. It is a tossup whether research should begin with the nature of the ghetto economy, the ghetto family, or the ghetto youth. But a great deal more exploration is needed of the ways in which ghetto youths differ from their nonghetto counterparts and which of these factors contribute to nonsuccess in labor markets.

a. What does the ghetto youth want? Can their aspirations be identified and generalized? What are the trade-offs between employment success and peer acceptance? Are these in conflict? What are ghetto youths' perceptions of opportunity? Are their aspirations primarily a consequence of their perceptions of opportunities or of their real preferences? Such data can be gathered only by extensive interviewing and surveying by psychologists.

b. What is the ghetto youth willing to do to achieve his aspirations? Is it lack of desire or a realistic estimate of low payoff that accounts for low self-investment? Is the choice between legitimate and illicit activity made emotionally or objectively? Is opportunity recognized and grasped? Only confronting samples of youth with differential opportunity situations or large-scale surveys comparing the reactions of those with identical characteristics in various opportunity circumstances can provide answers.

c. What is the ghetto youth capable of? Does the ghetto environment deprive one of essential skills and attitudes required for employment success? Is there a measureable difference in the willingness to work, the ability to perform simple tasks, the attention span, and similar factors between ghetto and nonghetto youth when controlled for race, education, and other factors? Comparative studies should be possible by occupation across ghetto and nonghetto settings.

7. Another related research dimension of the evolving ghetto neighborhood is the issue of those teenagers who succeed. Popularized autobiographies such as those by Malcolm X and Claude Brown are representative of individuals who have emerged from their ghetto origins and gone on to achieve economic and social success. Are the characteristics and patterns described in Chapter 4 as the ones that make for successful career development in the broader population the same ones that make for success in the ghetto alumni? A larger research effort should be focused on young adults with ghetto origins whose socioeconomic attainment might be stratified by successful college completion and career placement as well as stably employed blue-collar workers. A sample of such individuals could be analyzed on a retrospective basis by identifying family background, peer group associations as youth, and early teenage experiences in the ghetto labor market. This analysis of ghetto success would most likely reduce to a case-study approach and could very well build from the earlier literature cited in Goldstein. [26] Although the selected sample might represent a small proportion of the overall ghetto youth population, it would offer a basis for identifying factors and relationships where marginal impacts on the problem of ghetto youth unemployment might be made. What are the differential characteristics of the successful

and the unsuccessful? What were the differences in the opportunity structure? Where in the life continuum from home, neighborhood, school, larger community, and work did the essential variables of success come into play? Psychologists must add their skills to those of the sociologists, anthropologists, and economists in this search.

Data Sources

All of the above suggestions require significant data inputs for effective research design and output. A number of sources used in this monograph are representative of the type of data that is available. The 1970 census survey of sixty urban ghettos is one of the more promising sources for any kind of cross-sectional study. It contains a wealth of socioeconomic data that have not been effectively tapped on the basis of our literature search. Moreover, one might be able to piece together a "quasi" time series for select central cities.

A bona fide time series on the ghetto economy and unemployed teenagers is more problematic. A limited, aggregate series can be constructed from national data between 1967 and current Department of Labor data. Alternatives are microdata sources such as the National Longitudinal Survey (NLS) data. NLS data on the early work experience of teenagers and young adults is currently being analyzed by Adams, Mangum, et al., at the University of Utah. While the preliminary results are most promising for understanding youth unemployment as a whole, there is no breakdown available for central city or ghetto teenagers. This unfortunate gap suggests the Bureau of the Census Current Population Surveys as an alternative source of national data for central city youth. A city-specific series might be constructed from the more recent *Geographic Profile of Employment and Unemployment* series published by the Bureau of Labor Statistics, as well as occasional reports put out by regional BLS offices. A much larger sample would be required in ghetto labor markets to obtain statistically valid data on the phenomena in question.

But the aggregate and computerizable data sources will never do the job. Those in the irregular economy will never truthfully answer the questions of an official census taker. The probing will have to be done by those who engender trust. Ferman's Detroit activities prove it can be done, at least in some circumstances. Retrospective

99

case studies may produce relevant longitudinal data without awaiting the years necessary to accumulate current data. Students from ghetto backgrounds might be recruited to go back into their neighborhoods and trace from parents and acquaintances as well as from the individuals who can be found the postschool lives of ghetto-raised youth. The differential characteristics or random experiences accounting for success and failure might be determined on that basis. Such studies cannot be aggregated into a national data series, but often insight is all that is necessary for determining policy.

Employers are generally easier to study, but greater intensity is needed than will be reported by employers on either a voluntary or a compulsory self-reporting form. The modern preferences of researchers to sit at a computer terminal in a comfortable office manipulating aggregate data will have to give way to getting out into the street.

Experimental and Demonstration Efforts

Much can be learned through research. But research identifies problems, not solutions. Too often policy has flowed from gut feelings rather than from a base of researched knowledge. Yet research has often been sterile for lack of experiment with implied solutions. The supported work project cited above is an outstanding example of substantial public and private funds invested in trying out a solution indicated by basic research efforts. Comments early in this chapter about the potential for changed uses of the military, the civil service, the Job Corps, and other youth programs, for linkage with employers, and for the impact of more certain law enforcement cannot stop with research. They must be tried out in practice and proved or disproved in that expensive and painful crucible. Three experimental and demonstration efforts would appear to merit priority.

1. Career Education is the name of a current national movement to regularize in the schools the more positive aspects of the normal career development process described in the first section of Chapter 4. Starting in the elementary school or even earlier through parent training, work values and attitudes, career awareness, and career exploration, decision making, and career preparation are all intermingled with and provide motivation for academic learning. [27]

Though the majority of school districts now have some career education activities, the literature of the field is quiet on ghetto applications. An intensive application of the best of career education practices in one ghetto high school and its feeder middle or junior high and elementary schools could test the techniques and potential for career education, seeking to offset to some degree the limitations of the home and community environment.

2. Youth gangs obviously play an essential role, negative or positive, in the maturation of the central city youth. The efforts to combat juvenile deliquency of the 1950s and early 1960s sought to infiltrate these gangs and use them for positive reinforcement. Little is found of such efforts in the literature of more recent years. Can these informal associations so important to youth with weak family structures be channeled into a positive peer influence on employability and employment?

3. As noted above, one solution to ghetto youth unemployment may be to decentralize youth through the military, the Job Corps, the Young Adult Conservation Corps, decentralized public and subsidized housing, and other devices. The programs for the disadvantaged face the handicap that they have enrolled only youth from the commonly deficient backgrounds, but at least they are a potential route to geographical escape. The military is a somewhat better mixer of backgrounds and exposure to varied life styles. These institutions already tend toward the desired effect, but their potential is limited. Other more dramatic encouragements for outmigration of ghetto youth and their families need to be designed and demonstrated.

Concluding Comments

The unemployment dilemma for America's ghetto youth is a demanding social issue that is not unsolvable but that needs more concerted research and imaginative experiment. This monograph has identified and outlined many of the factors that are critical elements in this problem. An increased research and demonstration effort leading to appropriate public policy action has the potential of an enormous social payoff in the form of meaningful and dignified participation in urban society. Despite the growth of the social research industry, policy is still essentially designed according to gut feelings or the need for a political issue. The ghetto youth unemployment problem has been around for a long time and will not go away by itself, or soon, in any event. It is a fit subject for the best minds in economics, sociology, anthropology, and psychology, to name only a few disciplines. It will require research resources from government and foundations, but those costs will not be significant beside those of the unsolved problem or the ill-formed program. No more than marginal improvement can be expected from the best research and the best policy. But that margin is often the difference between the acceptable and the insufferable.

Notes

Chapter 1

1. Stanley L. Friedlander, *Unemployment in the Urban Core: An Analysis of Thirty Cities with Policy Recommendations* (New York: Praeger Publishers, 1972).

2. Sar Levitan and Robert Taggart, "Background Paper on the Job Crisis for Black Youth," in the Twentieth Century Fund Task Force on Employment Problems of Black Youth, *The Job Crisis for Black Youth* (New York: Praeger Publishers, 1971).

Chapter 2

1. Equal Employment Opportunity Commission, *Employment Profiles of Women and Minorities in 23 Metropolitan Areas, 1974,* Research Report No. 49, 1976 (Washington, D.C.: U.S. Government Printing Office, 1976).

2. U.S. Bureau of the Census, *Current Population Reports,* Series P-23, No. 37, "Social and Economic Characteristics of the Population in Metropolitan and Nonmetropolitan Areas: 1970 and 1960" (Washington, D.C.: U.S. Government Printing Office, 1971), and *Current Population Reports,* Series P-23, No. 55.

3. U.S. Bureau of the Census, *Census of Population: 1970 Employment Profiles of Selected Low-Income Areas,* Final Report PHC (3)-1, United States Summary—Urban Areas (Washington, D.C.: U.S. Government Printing Office, 1972).

4. U.S. Bureau of the Census, *Current Population Reports,* Series P-23, No. 18, "Characteristics of the South and East Los Angeles Areas: November 1965" (Washington, D.C.: U.S. Government Printing Office, 1966); *Current Population Reports,* Series P-23, No. 19, "Characteristics of Selected Neighborhoods in Cleveland, Ohio: April 1965" (Washington, D.C.: U.S. Government Printing Office, 1966); *Census of Population: 1970 Employment Profiles of Selected Low-Income Areas,* Los Angeles, Calif., Area II PHC (3)-18 (Washington, D.C.: U.S. Government Printing Office, 1972); *Census of Population: 1970 Employment Profiles of Selected Low-Income Areas,* Cleveland, Ohio, PHC (3)-29 (Washington, D.C.: U.S. Government Printing Office, 1972).

5. Martin S. Feldstein, *Lowering the Permanent Rate of Unemployment: A Study,* Joint Economic Committee Printing, 93 Cong., 1 sess., September 18, 1973 (Washington, D.C.: U.S. Government Printing Office, 1973).

6. Lowell E. Gallaway, "Unemployment Levels among Non-White Teenagers," *Journal of Business* 42, no. 3 (July 1969): 265-76.

7. Ralph Smith, "The Teenage Unemployment Problem—How Much Will Macro Policies Matter?" in Congressional Budget Office, *The Teenage Unemployment Problem: What Are the Options* (Washington, D.C.: U.S. Government Printing Office, 1976), pp. 7-17.

8. Sar Levitan and Robert Taggart, "Background Paper on the Job Crisis for Black Youth," in Twentieth Century Fund Task Force on Employment Problems of Black Youth, *The Job Crisis for Black Youth* (New York: Praeger Publishers, 1971).

9. Bernard Anderson, "Youth Unemployment Problems in the Inner City," in Congressional Budget Office, *The Teenage Unemployment Problem*; *What Are the Options* (Washington, D.C.: U.S. Government Printing Office, 1976), p. 25.

10. Christopher Jencks et al., "Efforts of Family Background, Test Scores, Personality Traits, and Schooling on Economic Success" (Final report to the National Institute of Education and to the Employment and Training Administration pursuant to Grant No. NIE-G-74-0077, April 1977).

11. *1970 Employment Profiles on Low-Income Areas*, United States Summary—Urban Areas.

Chapter 3

1. Wilbur R. Thompson, *A Preface to Urban Economics* (Baltimore: Johns Hopkins University Press, 1968).

2. A recent comprehensive survey by Bennett Harrison, "Ghetto Economic Development," *Journal of Economic Literature* 12, no. 1 (March 1974):1-37, was especially valuable for insights and references on the economics of the inner city. The following discussion is a brief survey that cites those parts of the literature that bear either directly or indirectly on youth employment problems in the inner city.

3. Edgar M. Hoover and Raymond Vernon, *Anatomy of a Metropolis* (Cambridge, Mass.: Harvard University Press, 1959).

4. John F. Kain, "The Distribution and Movement of Jobs and Industry," in J. Q. Wilson, ed., *The Metropolitan Enigma* (New York: Doubleday, 1970), pp. 1-43.

5. John R. Meyer, "Urban Transportation," in ibid., pp. 43-75.

6. Lowell E. Gallaway, "Urban Decay and the Labor Market," *Quarterly Review of Economics and Business* 7, no. 4 (Winter 1967): 7-16.

7. Christopher G. Gellner, "Occupational Characteristics of Urban Workers," *Monthly Labor Review* 84, no. 10 (November 1961): 21-32.

8. Marjorie C. Brazer, "Economic and Social Disparities between Central Cities and Their Suburbs," *Land Economics* 43, no. 3 (August 1967): 294-302, quote on p. 294.

9. Lester C. Thurow, *Poverty and Discrimination* (Washington, D.C.: Brookings Institution, 1969).

10. Anthony Downs, *Urban Problems and Prospects* (Chicago: Markham, 1970).

11. Thomas Vietorisz and Bennett Harrison, *The Economic Development of Harlem* (New York: Praeger Publishers, 1970).

12. William K. Tabb, *The Political Economy of the Black Ghetto* (New York: Norton, 1970).

13. Sar Levitan, Garth Mangum, and Robert Taggart, *Economic Opportunity in the Ghetto: The Partnership of Government and Business* (Baltimore: Johns Hopkins University Press, 1970).

14. Edward C. Banfield, *The Unheavenly City* (Boston: Little, Brown, and Company, 1970).

15. Edward C. Banfield, *The Unheavenly City Revisited* (Boston: Little, Brown, and Company, 1974).

16. Bennett Harrison, *Urban Economic Development* (Washington, D.C.: Urban Institute, 1974), p. 6.

17. Anthony Downs, *Opening up the Suburbs: An Urban Strategy for America* (New Haven: Yale University Press, 1973).

18. William C. Baer, "On the Death of Cities," *Public Interest*, No. 45 (Fall 1976), pp. 3-19.

19. Edward Kalachek, *The Youth Labor Market*, Policy Papers in Human Resource and Industrial Relations No. 12 (Ann Arbor: University of Michigan and National Manpower Policy Task Force, January 1969).

20. Stanley L. Friedlander, *Unemployment in the Urban Core: An Analysis of Thirty Cities with Policy Recommendations* (New York: Praeger Publishers, 1972).

21. Harrison, *Urban Economic Development*.

22. Ibid.

23. U.S. Bureau of the Census, *Current Population Reports*, Series P-23, No. 55, "Social and Economic Characteristics of Metropolitan and Nonmetropolitan Areas, 1974 and 1970" (Washington, D.C.: U.S. Government Printing Office, 1975).

24. This most current year unfortunately coincided with the national recession of 1974-75, although the unemployment consequences of that recession in central cities appear to have been greatest in 1975. The overall unemployment rate in cities increased slightly from 5.9 percent in 1973 to 6.5 percent in 1974; it then jumped to 9.6 percent in 1975. Central city unemployment rates for teenagers also reflected a much greater severity in 1975; this rate went from 18.6 percent in 1973 to 19.3 percent in 1974 and then up to 24.5 percent in 1975. This seems to be consistent with a 1975 second-quarter peak in unemployment rates reported by Janice Neipert Hedges, "Youth Unemployment in the 1974-1975 Recession," *Monthly Labor Review* 99, no. 1 (January 1976): 49-56.

25. Diane Westcott, "Youth in the Labor Force: An Area Study," *Monthly Labor Review* 99, no. 7 (July 1976): 3-9.

26. Harold F. Goldsmith and Edward G. Stockwell, "Interrelationships of Occupational Selectivity Patterns among City, Suburban, and Fringe Areas of Major Metropolitan Areas," *Land Economics* 45, no. 2 (May 1969): 194-205.

27. Diane Westcott, "The Nation's Youth: An Employment Perspective," *Worklife* 2, no. 6 (June 1977): 13-19.

28. U.S. Bureau of the Census, *Census of Population: 1970 Employment Profiles of Selected Low-Income Areas*, Final Report PHC (3)-1, United States Summary—Urban Areas (Washington, D.C.: U.S. Government Printing Office, 1972).

29. Sheldon Danziger and Michael Weinstein, "Employment Location and Wage Rates of Poverty-Area Residents," *Journal of Urban Economics*, 3, no. 2 (April 1976): 127-45, quotes on p. 128.

30. Shane Davies and David Huff, "Impact of Ghettoization on Black Employment," *Economic Geography* 48, no. 4 (October 1972): 421-27.

31. Friedlander, *Unemployment in the Urban Core*, p. 128.

32. David M. Gordon, *Theories of Poverty and Underemployment* (Lexington, Mass.: D. C. Heath, 1972).

33. James F. Ragan, "Minimun Wages and the Youth Labor Market," *Review of Economics and Statistics* 59, no. 2 (May 1977): 129-36.

34. Alan Fisher, "The Problem of Teenage Unemployment" (Ph.D. dissertation, University of California, Berkeley, August 1973).

35. Friedlander, *Unemployment in the Urban Core*, pp. 141-42.

36. Bennett Harrison, "Education and Underemployment in the Urban Ghetto," *American Economic Review* 62, no. 5 (December 1972):796-812, quote on p. 811.

37. Paul Osterman, "The Structure of the Labor Market for Young Men" (mimeographed manuscript, Department of Economics, Boston University, 1977).

38. Bennett Harrison, *Public Employment and Urban Poverty* (Washington, D.C.: Urban Institute, 1971).

39. Roger Noll, "Metropolitan Employment and Population Distribution and the Conditions of the Urban Poor," in John P. Crecine, ed., *Financing the Metropolis* (Beverly Hills, Calif.: Sage Publications, 1970).

40. Westcott, "The Nation's Youth," pp. 13-19.

41. Gelvin Stevenson, "Determinants of the Occupational Employment of Black and White Male Teenagers" (Ph.D. dissertation, Washington University, June 1973).

42. Eleanor H. Bernert, *America's Children* (New York: John Wiley and Sons, 1958).

43. John Korbel, "Labor Force Entry and Attachment of Young People," *Journal of American Statistical Association* 16 (March 1966): 117-27.

44. These data are from the U.S. Bureau of the Census, *Current Population Reports*, Series P-60, No. 102, "Characteristics of the Population below the Poverty Level: 1974" (Washington, D.C.: U.S. Government Printing Office, 1976).

45. Bureau of the Census, *1970 Census* and *1970 Employment Profiles of Selected Low-Income Areas*.

46. Grey J. Duncan and James N. Morgan, eds., *Five Thousand American Families—Patterns of Economic Progress*. Volumes 1, 2, 3, 4, 5 (Ann Arbor: Institute for Social Research, 1976).

47. Daniel Hill and Martha Hill, "Older Children and Splitting Off," in ibid., 4: 118-26.

Chapter 4

1. Eli Ginzberg et al., *Occupational Choice* (New York: Columbia University Press, 1951); Samuel H. Osipow, "Implications for Career Education of Research and Theory on Career Development" (Paper prepared for the National Conference on Career Education for Deans of Colleges of Education, Columbus, Ohio, Center for Vocational and Technical Education, Ohio State University, 1972); Anne Roe, "Perspectives on Vocational Development," in *Perspectives on Vocational Development*. John M. Whiteley and Arthur Resnikoff, eds. (Washington, D.C.: American Personnel and Guidance Association, 1972), pp. 61-82; David V. Tiedeman and Robert P. O'Hara, "Career Development: Choice and Adjustment, (Mimeographed, New York: College Entrance Examination Board, 1963).

2. Donald E. Super, "Vocational Development Theory: Persons, Positions, and Processes," *Counseling Psychologist* 1, No. 1 (1969): 2-9; Anne Roe, "A Psychological Study of Eminent Psychologists and Anthropologists and a Comparison with Biological and Physical Scientists," *Psychological Monographs* 67, no. 2 (1953); R. A. Schutz and D. H. Blocker, "Self-Satisfaction and Level of Occupational Choice," *Personnel and Guidance Journal* 40 (1961): 595-98; John L. Holland, "Some Explorations of a Theory of Vocational Choice: I. One and Two-Year Longitudinal Studies," *Psychological Monographs* 76, no. 26 (1962): 1-49; John L. Holland, "Explanations of a Theory of Vocational Choice and Achievement: II. A Four-Year Prediction Study," *Psychological Reports* 12, no. 2 (1963): 547-94.

3. Barbara Inhelder and Jean Piaget, *The Growth of Logical Thinking from Childhood to Adolescence* (New York: Basic Books, 1958).

4. David A. Schulz, "Coming up as a Boy in the Ghetto," in Doris Wilkinson and Donald L. Taylor, eds., *The Black Male in America* (Chicago: Nelson Hall, 1971), pp. 7-32.

5. Eric Erikson, *Childhood and Society* (New York: Norton, 1963).

6. Ginzberg et al., *Occupational Choice.*

7. Erickson, *Childhood and Society.*

8. Ibid.

9. Rupert Evans, Kenneth Hoyt, and Garth Mangum, *Career Education in the Middle/Junior High School* (Salt Lake City: Olympus Publishing Co., 1973).

10. Super, "Vocational Development Theory."

11. Robert J. Havinghurst, *Human Development and Education* (New York: Longmans, Green, and Company, 1953).

12. Tiedeman and O'Hara, "Career Development."

13. Carol B. Stack, *All Our Kin* (New York: Harper and Row, 1974).

14. Lee Rainwater, "Identity Processes in the Family," in Robert Staples, ed., *The Black Family* (Belmont, Calif.: Wadsworth Publishing Company, 1971), pp. 257-61, quote on p. 261.

15. Camille Jeffers, *Living Poor* (Ann Arbor, Mich.: Ann Arbor Publishers, 1967).

16. William Moore, Jr., *The Vertical Ghetto* (New York: Random House, 1969).

17. Lee Rainwater, *Behind Ghetto Walls* (Chicago: Aldine Publishing Company, 1970).

18. Daniel P. Moynihan, "The Tangle of Pathology: The Moynihan Report," in Staples, ed., *Black Family,* pp. 37-57.

19. Laura Carper, "The Negro Family and the Moynihan Report," in ibid., pp. 65-71, quote on p. 68.

20. Robert R. Bell, "The Related Importance of Mother and Wife Roles," in ibid., pp. 248-56.

21. Ulf Hannerz, *Soulside* (New York: Columbia University Press, 1969).

22. Joyce A. Ladner, *Tomorrow's Tomorrow. The Black Woman* (Garden City, N.Y.: Doubleday, 1972).

23. Constance Kamil and Norma J. Radin, "Class Differences in the Socialization Practices of Negro Mothers," in Staples, ed., *Black Family,* pp. 235-47.

24. Rainwater, *Behind Ghetto Walls.*

25. Schulz, "Coming up as a Boy in the Ghetto," pp. 7-32.

26. Sar A. Levitan and Robert Taggart, "Background Paper on the Job Crisis for Black Youth," in Twentieth Century Fund Task Force on Employment Problems of Black Youth, *The Job Crisis for Black Youth* (New York: Praeger Publishers, 1971).

27. Schulz, "Coming up as a Boy," p. 13.

28. Hannerz, *Soulside.*

29. Schulz, "Coming up as a Boy."

30. Robert Staples, "The Myth of the Black Matriarchy," in Staples, ed., *Black Family.* pp. 149-58, quote on p. 155.

31. Schulz, "Coming up as a Boy."

32. Moynihan, "The Tangle of Pathology."

33. Harland Padfield and Roy Williams, *Stay Where You Were* (Philadelphia: J. P. Lippincott Company, 1973).

34. Elliot Liebow, *Talley's Corner: A Study of Negro Streetcorner Men* (Boston: Little, Brown, and Company, 1967).

35. Stack, *All Our Kin.*

36. Liebow, *Talley's Corner.*

37. Nathan Caplan, "The New Ghetto Man: A Review of Empirical Studies," in Wilkinson and Taylor, eds., *Black Male,* pp. 309-25.

38. Joseph S. Hines, "Some Work-Related Cultural Deprivations in Lower-Class Negro Youth," in Staples, ed., *Black Family,* pp. 262–66.

39. Meyer Winberg, *Minority Students: A Research Appraisal* (Washington, D.C.: U.S. Department of Health, Education, and Welfare, National Institute of Education, 1977).

40. Ibid.

41. Barry Silverstein and Ronald Krate, *Children of the Dark Ghetto* (New York: Praeger Publishers, 1975).

42. Paul Bullock, *Aspirations vs. Opportunity: "Careers" in the Inner City* (Ann Arbor, Mich.: Institute of Labor and Industrial Relations, 1973).

43. James B. Conant, *Slums and Suburbs* (New York: New American Library, 1961).

44. Florence Howe and Paul Lauter, "How the School System is Rigged for Failure," in Richard Edwards, Michael Reich, and Thomas Weisskopf, eds., *The Capitalist System* (Englewood Cliffs, N.J.: Prentice-Hall, 1972).

45. James N. Porter, "Race, Socialization, Maturity in Educational Attainment," *American Sociological Review* 39 (June 1974): 303–16.

46. Howe and Lauter, "School System."

47. U.S. Department of Labor, *Manpower Report to the President, 1975* (Washington, D.C.; U.S. Government Printing Office, 1975).

48. Bullock, *Aspirations vs. Opportunity.*

49. Rainwater, "Identity Processes."

50. Schulz, "Coming up as a Boy."

51. Ibid.

52. Richard C. Stephens and Duane C. McBride, "Becoming a Street Addict," *Human Resources* 35 (Spring 1976): 87–93.

53. Herbert C. Ellis and Stanley M. Newman, "Gouster, Ivy Leaguer, Hustler, Conservative, Mockman, and Continental: A Functional Analysis of Six Ghetto Roles," in Eleanor B. Leacock, ed., *The Culture of Poverty, A Critique* (New York: Simon and Schuster, 1971).

54. C. Jack Friedman, Frederica Mann, and Albert Friedman, "A Profile of Juvenile Street Gang Members," *Adolescence* 10 (Winter 1975): 563–607.

55. Ellis and Newman, "Gouster, Ivy Leaguer, Hustler."

56. William McCord, John Howard, Bernard Frieberg, and Edwin Harwood, *Life Styles in the Black Ghetto* (New York: Norton, 1969).

57. Nathan Caplan, "Competency among Hard-to-Employ Youths" (Mimeo, Washington, D.C.: Manpower Administration, U.S. Department of Labor, 1973).

58. Ladner, *Tomorrow's Tomorrow.*

59. Ibid., p. 188.

60. Joseph S. Hines, "Some Work-Related Cultural Deprivations in Lower-Class Negro Youth," in Staples, ed., *Black Family,* pp. 262–66.

61. Louis A. Ferman, *Disadvantaged Youth: Problems of Job Placement, Job Creation, and Job Development* (Ann Arbor, Mich.: University of Michigan Press, 1967).

62. Caplan, "Competency among Hard-to Employ Youths."

63. Ladner, *Tomorrow's Tomorrow.*

64. Schulz, "Coming up as a Boy."

65. Julius Hudson. "The Hustling Ethic," in Thomas Kochman, ed., *Rappin' and Stylin' Out* (Champagne-Urbana: University of Illinois Press, 1972), p. 417.

66. Murray Binderman, Dennis Wepman, and Ronald Newman, "A Portrait of 'the Life'," *Urban Life,* July 4, 1976, pp. 213–30.

67. Louis Ferman, "The Irregular Economy: Urban Adaptation to Unemployment" (Final Report NIMH, No. 55R01-MH26105-02, October 1977).

68. Bullock, *Aspirations vs. Opportunity*, p. 99.
69. Hudson, "The Hustling Ethic."
70. Schulz, "Coming up as a Boy."
71. Kenneth Clark, *Dark Ghetto* (New York: Harper and Row, 1965), p. 13.
72. U.S. Department of Labor, *Manpower Report to the President, 1971* (Washington, D.C.: U.S. Government Printing Office, 1971), pp. 92-100, citing a study by Stanley Friedlander of the Conservation of Human Resources Staff, Columbia University, under contract with the Department of Labor, Manpower Administration.
73. Michael Schwartz and George Henderson, "The Culture of Unemployment: Some Notes on Negro Children," in A. B. Shostak and W. Camberg, eds., *Blue Collar World: Studies of the American Worker* (Englewood Cliffs, N.J.: Prentice-Hall, 1964).
74. Paul Osterman, "The Structure of the Labor Market for Young Men" (mimeographed manuscript, Department of Economics, Boston University, 1977).
75. Liebow, *Talley's Corner*.
76. Caplan, "The New Ghetto Man."
77. Claude Brown, *Manchild in the Promised Land* (New York: MacMillan Company, 1965).
78. Malcolm X, *The Autobiography of Malcolm X* (New York: Grove Press, 1964).
79. Claude Brown, *The Children of Ham* (New York: Stein and Day, 1973).

Chapter 5

1. Sar A. Levitan and Karen Cleary Alderman, *Warriors at Work* (San Francisco: Sage Publications, 1977).
2. Garth L. Mangum and Lowell Glenn, *Employing the Disadvantaged in the Federal Civil Service*, Policy Paper in Human Resources and Industrial Relations, No. 13 (Ann Arbor, Mich.: Institute of Industrial Relations, University of Michigan and Wayne State University, 1969).
3. Garth L. Mangum and John Walsh, *A Decade of Manpower Development and Training* (Salt Lake City, Utah: Olympus Publishing Company, 1973).
4. Marion W. Pines and James H. Morlock, *CETA Program Models: Work Experiences Perspectives*, forthcoming by Employment and Training Administration (Washington, D.C.: U.S. Department of Labor, 1978).
5. David Jeffrey, "Regional Fluctuations in Unemployment within the U.S. Urban Economic System: A Study of the Spatial Impact of Short Term Economic Change," *Economic Geography* 50, no. 2 (April 1974): 111-23.
6. Paul Osterman, *The Structure of the Labor Market for Young Men* (mimeographed manuscript, Department of Economics, Boston University, 1977).
7. Louis Ferman, "The Irregular Economy: Urban Adaptation to Unemployment" (Final Report NIMH, No. 55R01-MH26105-02, October 1977).
8. Stanley P. Stephenson, "The Economics of Youth Job Search Behavior," *Review of Economics and Statistics* 58 (February 1976): 104-11.
9. Julius Shiskin, *Information Memorandum on Highlights from a Special Survey of the Unemployed* (Washington, D.C.: U.S. Department of Labor, August 1977).
10. Sar Levitan and Robert Taggart, "Background Paper on Job Crisis for Black Youth," in Twentieth Century Task Force on Employment Problems of Black Youth, *The Job Crisis for Black Youth* (New York: Praeger Publishers, 1971).
11. Peter Doeringer and Michael Piore, *Internal Labor Markets and Manpower Analysis* (Lexington, Mass., D. C. Heath, 1971).

12. Arvil V. Adams, Garth L. Mangum, et al., "The Lingering Crises of Youth Unemployment: New Perspectives from Longitudinal Data (Research report submitted to Upjohn Institute, December 1977).

13. Manpower Demonstration Research Corporation, *Analysis of Nine Month Interviews: Results of an Early Sample* (Madison, Wis.: Mathematical Policy Research and the Institute for Research on Poverty, 1977).

14. Duane E. Leigh, "The Occupational Mobility of Young Men, 1965-1970," *Industrial and Labor Relations Review* 30 (October 1976): 68-78.

15. Robert E. Hall and Richard Kasten, "Occupational Success among Young Men," *American Economic Review* 66, no. 2 (May 1976): 309-15.

16. Mary Corcoran, Christopher Jencks, and Michael Olnech, "The Effects of Family Background and Earnings," *American Economic Review* 66, no. 2 (May 1976): 430-35.

17. Bennett Harrison, *Urban Economic Development* (Washington, D.C.: Urban Institute, 1974).

18. Linda Nasif Edwards, "School Retention of Teenagers over the Business Cycle," *Journal of Human Resources* 11, no. 2 (Spring 1976): 200-208.

19. A. J. H. Dean, "Unemployment among School Leavers: An Analysis of the Problem," *National Institute of Economic Review,* (November 1976), pp. 63-68.

20. Bureau of Labor Statistics, New York Office, *The New York Puerto Rican: Pattern of Work Experience* (Regional Report, no. 19, May 1971).

21. D. P. Slesinger, "Occupational and Land Use Changes in a Selected Central City Area of Milwaukee," *Land Economics* 48 (1972): 290-97.

22. Harold M. Rose, "The Spatial Development of Black Residential Subsystems," *Economic Geography* 48, no. 1 (January 1972): 43-65.

23. R. A. Cloward and L. E. Ohlin, *Deliquency and Opportunity* (New York: Free Press, 1960).

24. Jon Bradshaw, "Savage Skulls," *Esquire Magazine,* June 1977, pp. 74-82.

25. Allen M. Cole and Charles W. Turner, "Effects on Crime Rates of Changing Birth Orders during the Post World War II Baby Boom" (Discussion paper, Department of Psychology, University of Utah, presented at the Western Psychological Association, Seattle, Wash., April 22, 1977).

26. Bernard Goldstein, *Low Income Youth in Urban Areas* (New York: Holt, Rinehart, Winston, 1967).

27. Kenneth Hoyt et al., *Career Education: What It Is and How To Do It* (Salt Lake City, Utah: Olympus Research Corporation, 1972).

Index

Academic achievement of ghetto children, 72

Adolescence, career development in, 61

Age composition: black teenage components of, 17; of central cities, 17; and minority youth concentration, 19; and youth share of city population, 18

Baby boom: effect of, on urban youth population, 16; effects of, on teenage labor force, 14; and ghetto teenagers, 2; and incidence of crime, 96; and interaction with urban crisis, 5; peaks in, 14; relationship of, to teen unemployment rates, 14

Career development: in adolescence, 61; content of, 57; differing paths of, 81; in ghetto, 64; and interaction with biological and psychological growth, 57; in later childhood, 59; as lifelong process, 57; among middle class, 57; in preadolescence, 60; research on, 57; work values in, 57; of young adults, 63

Career education, current national movement in, 100

Child: female, in ghetto, 76; socialization of, in ghetto, 73

Competencies of street youth, 76

Comprehensive Employment and Training Act (CETA): impact of, on unemployed urban youth, 86; and public works employment, 86

Credentials gap: effect of, on minority teenagers, 4; and entry-level jobs, 28; and job mismatch, 28; and job vacancies, 28

Crime: in ghetto, 89; and high-risk age groups, 97; and illegal employment opportunities, 96; relationship of, to age structure, 96; and youth gangs, 101

Decision-making skills, development of, 62

Dope peddlers, interviews with, 78

Drug addiction, experience with, 82

Drug addicts, interviews with, 75

Dual labor markets: entry barriers in, 41; high turnover in, 91; and peripheral workers, 91; and primary sector jobs, 41; and unions, 41

Dysfunctional life style in urban ghetto, 95

Education: displacement effects of, 43, 44; employers' entry requirements, 93; gaps in, 43; in ghetto areas, 43; as part of urban policy, 85; and skill requirements in entry-level jobs, 93

Library of Congress Cataloging in Publication Data

Mangum, Garth L.
    Coming of age in the ghetto.
    (Policy studies in employment and welfare; no. 33)
    Includes index.
    1.   Afro-American youth—Employment.   2.   Spanish-
Americans in the United States—Employment.
I.   Seninger, Stephen F., joint author.   II.   Ford
Foundation.   III.   Title.
E188.86.M36   331.6′3′96073   78-8422
ISBN 0-8018-2125-8